Integrated Chinese

中文聽說讀寫

Traditional Character Edition
Workbook

Tao-chung Yao and Yuehua Liu
Yea-fen Chen, Liangyan Ge and Xiaojun Wang

Cheng & Tsui Company

Copyright © 1997 Tao-chung Yao, Yuehua Liu,
Yea-fen Chen, Liangyan Ge and Xiaojun Wang

All rights reserved. No part of this publication may be reproduced or transmitted in any form or by any means, electronic or mechanical, including photocopy, recording, or any information storage or retrieval system, without written permission from the publisher.

First edition

Cheng & Tsui Company
25 West Street
Boston, MA 02111-1268 USA

Traditional Character Edition
ISBN 0-88727-264-9

Companion textbooks, character workbooks and audio tapes are also available from the publisher.

Printed in the United States of America

PUBLISHER'S NOTE

The Cheng & Tsui Company is pleased to announce the most recent addition to its Asian Language Series, *Integrated Chinese*. This entirely new course program for the beginning to advanced student of Mandarin Chinese will incorporate textbooks, workbooks, character workbooks, teaching aids, audio tapes, video tapes, CD-ROM computer programs and interactive multimedia programs. Field-tested since 1994, this series has been very well received. It is our intention to keep it a dynamic product by continuing to add, revise and refine the content as we get your valuable feedback.

This series seeks to train students in all four language skills: listening, speaking, reading and writing. It utilizes a variety of pedagogical approaches—grammar translation, audio-lingual, direct method, total physical response—to achieve the desired results. Because no two Chinese language programs are the same, *Integrated Chinese* provides those classes that cover the lessons more speedily with additional material in the form of Supplementary Vocabulary. The Supplementary Vocabulary section, however, is purely optional.

The *C&T Asian Language Series* is designed to publish and widely distribute quality language texts as they are completed by such leading institutions as the Beijing Language Institute, as well as other significant works in the field of Asian languages developed in the United States and elsewhere.

We welcome readers' comments and suggestions concerning the publications in this series. Please contact the following members of the Editorial Board:

Professor Shou-hsin Teng, Chief Editor
3 Coach Lane, Amherst, MA 01002

Dana Scott Bourgerie
Asian and Near Eastern Languages, Brigham Young University, Provo, UT 84602

Professor Samuel Cheung
Dept. of Oriental Languages, University of California, Berkeley, CA 94720

Professor Ying-che Li
Dept. of East Asian Languages, University of Hawaii, Honolulu, HI 96822

Professor Timothy Light
Office of the Provost, Western Michigan University, Kalamazoo, MI 49008

Cheng and Tsui Language Series

Editorial Board

Shou-hsin Teng, Chief Editor

Dana Scott Bourgerie

Samuel Cheung

Ying-che Li

Timothy Light

PREFACE

In designing *Integrated Chinese, Level One* workbook exercises, we strove to give equal emphasis to the students' listening, speaking, reading, and writing skills. There are different difficulty levels in order to provide variety and flexibility to suit different curriculum needs. Teachers should assign the exercises at their discretion; they should not feel pressured into using all of them and should feel free to use them out of sequence, if appropriate. Moreover, teachers can complement this workbook with their own exercises.

I. Listening Comprehension

All too often listening comprehension is sacrificed in a formal classroom setting because of time constraint. Students tend to focus their time and energies on the mastery of a few grammar points. This workbook tries to remedy this imbalance by including a substantial number of listening comprehension exercises.

There are two categories of listening exercises; both can be done on the students' own time or in the classroom. In either case, it is important to have the instructor review the students' answers for accuracy.

The first category of listening exercises consists of a tape recording of each lesson. For the exercises to be meaningful, students should *first* study the vocabulary list, *then* listen to the recordings *before* attempting to read the texts. The questions are provided to help students' aural understanding of the texts and to test their reading comprehension.

The second category of listening exercises consists of a tape recording of three or more mini-dialogues or solo narrations. These exercises are designed to recycle the vocabulary and grammar points introduced in the new lesson. Some of the exercises are significantly more difficult since students are asked to choose among several possible answers. These exercises, therefore, should be assigned towards the end of a lesson, when the students have become familiar with the content of the texts.

II. Speaking Exercises

Here, too, there are two types of exercises. However, they are designed for different levels of proficiency within each lesson and should be assigned at the appropriate time. In the first type, to help students apply their newly-acquired vocabulary and grammatical understanding to meaningful communication, we ask concrete, personal questions related to their daily lives. These questions require a one or two sentence answer. By stringing together short questions and answers, students can construct their own mini-dialogues, practice in pairs or take turns asking or answering the questions.

Once they have gained confidence, students can progress to more difficult questions where they are invited to express opinions on a number of topics. Typically, these questions are abstract, so the students will gradually learn to express their opinions and give their answers in paragraph-length discourse. As the school year progresses, these types of questions should take up more class discussion time. Because this second type of speaking exercise is quite challenging, it should be attempted only *after* students are well-grounded in the grammar and vocabulary of a particular lesson. This is usually *not immediately* after completing the first part of the speaking exercises.

III. Reading Comprehension

There are three to four passages for reading comprehension in each lesson. The first passage—usually short and related to the lesson at hand—recycles vocabulary and grammar points.

The second passage consists of slightly modified authentic materials, such as print advertisements, announcements, school diplomas, newspaper articles, etc. This passage may contain some unfamiliar vocabulary. The purpose of these materials is to train students to scan for useful information and not to let the appearance of a few new words distract them from comprehending the "big picture." Here, the teacher has a particularly important role to play in easing the students' anxiety about unfamiliar vocabulary. Teachers should encourage the student to ask: What do I really need to look for in a job announcement, a personal ad, or movie listings? Students should refer frequently to the questions to help them decipher these materials and should resist looking up every new word in their dictionary.

IV. Writing and Grammar Exercises

A. Grammar and Usage

These drills and exercises are designed to solidify the students' grasp of important grammar points. Through brief exchanges, students answer questions using specific grammatical forms or are given sentences to complete. By providing context for these exercises, students gain a clearer understanding of the grammar points and will not treat them as simple mechanical repetition drills.

Towards the last quarter of the lessons, students are introduced to increasingly sophisticated and abstract vocabulary. Corresponding exercises help them to grasp the nuances of new words. For example, synonyms are a source of great difficulty, so exercises are provided to help students distinguish between them.

B. Translation

Translation has been a tool for language teaching throughout the ages, and positive student feedback confirms our belief that it continues to play an important role. The exercises we have devised serve to reinforce two primary areas: one, to get students to apply specific grammatical structures; two, to allow students to build on their ever-increasing vocabulary. Ultimately, our hope is that this dual-pronged approach will enable students to understand that it takes more than just literal translation to convey an idea in a foreign language.

C. Composition

This is the culmination of the written exercises and is where students learn to express themselves in writing. Many of the topics overlap with those used in oral practice. We expect that students will find it easier to put in writing what they have already learned to express orally.

TABLE OF CONTENTS

Introduction   Pronunciation Exercises

PART ONE

I. Single Words. (Listen carefully and circle the correct answer.)

A: Initials

1.	a.	pà	b.	bà
2.	a.	pí	b.	bí
3.	a.	nán	b.	mán
4.	a.	fú	b.	hú
5.	a.	tīng	b.	dīng
6.	a.	tǒng	b.	dǒng
7.	a.	nán	b.	lán
8.	a.	niàn	b.	liàn
9.	a.	gàn	b.	kàn
10.	a.	kuì	b.	huì
11.	a.	kǎi	b.	hǎi
12.	a.	kuā	b.	huā
13.	a.	jiān	b.	qiān
14.	a.	yú	b.	qú
15.	a.	xiāng	b.	shāng
16.	a.	chú	b.	rú
17.	a.	zhá	b.	zá
18.	a.	zì	b.	cì
19.	a.	sè	b.	shè
20.	a.	sè	b.	cè
21.	a.	zhǒng	b.	jiǒng
22.	a.	shēn	b.	sēn
23.	a.	rù	b.	lù

B: Finals

1.   a. tuō   b. tōu
2.   a. guǒ   b. gǒu
3.   a. duò   b. dòu
4.   a. diū   b. dōu
5.   a. liú   b. lóu
6.   a. yǒu   b. yǔ
7.   a. nǔ   b. nǚ
8.   a. lú   b. lǘ
9.   a. yuán   b. yán
10.   a. píng   b. pín
11.   a. làn   b. luàn
12.   a. huán   b. hán
13.   a. fèng   b. fèn
14.   a. bèng   b. bèn
15.   a. lún   b. léng
16.   a. bīn   b. bīng
17.   a. kěn   b. kǔn
18.   a. héng   b. hóng
19.   a. téng   b. tóng
20.   a. kēng   b. kōng
21.   a. pàn   b. pàng
22.   a. fǎn   b. fǎng
23.   a. dǎn   b. dǎng
24.   a. mín   b. míng
25.   a. pēn   b. pān
26.   a. rén   b. rán
27.   a. mán   b. mén

C: Tones: First and Fourth (Level and Falling)

1. a. bō   b. bó
2. a. pān   b. pàn
3. a. wù   b. wū
4. a. tà   b. tā
5. a. qū   b. qù
6. a. sì   b. sī
7. a. fēi   b. fèi
8. a. duì   b. duī
9. a. xià   b. xiā
10. a. yā   b. yà

D: Tones: Second and Third (Low and Rising)

1. a. mǎi   b. mái
2. a. fǎng   b. fáng
3. a. dá   b. dǎ
4. a. tú   b. tǔ
5. a. nǐ   b. ní
6. a. wú   b. wǔ
7. a. bǎ   b. bá
8. a. shí   b. shǐ
9. a. huǐ   b. huí
10. a. féi   b. fěi
11. a. mǎ   b. má
12. a. dí   b. dǐ
13. a. láo   b. lǎo
14. a. gé   b. gě
15. a. zhǐ   b. zhí

E: Tones: All four tones

1.   a. bà   b. bā

2.   a. pí   b. pì

3.   a. méi   b. měi

4.   a. wēn   b. wěn

5.   a. zǎo   b. zāo

6.   a. yōu   b. yóu

7.   a. guāng   b. guǎng

8.   a. zhuāng   b. zhuàng

9.   a. qì   b. qí

10. a. mào   b. máo

11. a. bǔ   b. bù

12. a. kuàng   b. kuāng

13. a. jú   b. jǔ

14. a. qiáng   b. qiāng

15. a. xián   b. xiān

16. a. yǒng   b. yòng

17. a. zú   b. zū

18. a. cí   b. cǐ

19. a. suī   b. suí

20. a. zhèng   b. zhēng

21. a. chòu   b. chóu

22. a. shuāi   b. shuài

23. a. wǒ   b. wò

24. a. yào   b. yáo

25. a. huī   b. huì

26. a. rú   b. rù

27. a. rén   b. rèn

F: Comprehensive Exercise

1. a. jiā   b. zhā
2. a. chuí   b. qué
3. a. chǎng   b. qiǎng
4. a. xū   b. shū
5. a. shuǐ   b. xuě
6. a. zǎo   b. zhǎo
7. a. zǎo   b. cǎo
8. a. sōu   b. shōu
9. a. tōu   b. tuō
10. a. dǒu   b. duǒ
11. a. duǒ   b. zuǒ
12. a. mǎi   b. měi
13. a. shào   b. xiào
14. a. chóu   b. qiú
15. a. yuè   b. yè
16. a. jiǔ   b. zhǒu
17. a. nǔ   b. nǚ
18. a. zhú   b. jú
19. a. jì   b. zì
20. a. liè   b. lüè
21. a. jīn   b. zhēn
22. a. xiǔ   b. shǒu
23. a. kǔn   b. hěn
24. a. shǎo   b. xiǎo
26. a. zhǎng   b. jiǎng
27. a. qū   b. chū

II. Tone Combination Exercise.
(You will hear one word at a time. Please write down it's tones in the blank. Use 1-4 for the four tones, and 5 for neutral tones.)

Example: If you hear the word "Zhōngwén," you write "1 2" on the blank.

A:

1. _____	11. _____	21. _____
2. _____	12. _____	22. _____
3. _____	13. _____	23. _____
4. _____	14. _____	24. _____
5. _____	15. _____	25. _____
6. _____	16. _____	26. _____
7. _____	17. _____	27. _____
8. _____	18. _____	28. _____
9. _____	19. _____	29. _____
10. _____	20. _____	30. _____

B:

1. _____	11. _____	21. _____
2. _____	12. _____	22. _____
3. _____	13. _____	23. _____
4. _____	14. _____	24. _____
5. _____	15. _____	25. _____
6. _____	16. _____	26. _____
7. _____	17. _____	27. _____
8. _____	18. _____	28. _____
9. _____	19. _____	29. _____
10. _____	20. _____	30. _____

PART TWO

I. Initials and Simple Finals:

Please fill in the blanks with appropriate initials or simple finals.

A.1. ___a	A.2. p___	A.3. ___u	A.4. l___
B.1. f___	B.2. n___	B.3. ___i	B.4. ___u
C.1. ___a	C.2. l___	C.3. l___	C.4. ___u
D.1. ___u	D.2. t___	D.3. n___	D.4. n___
E.1. ___e	E.2. ___u	E.3. ___a	
F.1. g___	F.2. k___	F.3. h___	
G.1. ___u	G.2. ___i	G.3. ___u	
H.1. j___	H.2. q___	H.3. x___	
I.1. ___a	I.2. ___e	I.3. ___i	I.4. ___ü
J.1. ___u	J.2. c___	J.3. ___u	J.4. ___i
K.1. ___i	K.2. s___	K.3. ___a	K.4. q___
L.1. ___a	L.2. ___i	L.3. s___	L.4. ___u
M.1. c___	M.2. ___i	M.3. ___u	M.4. ___a
N.1. ___u	N.2. r___	N.3. ch___	N.4. ___e

II. Tones:

Please listen to the tape and mark the correct tone marks.

A.1. he	A.2. ma	A.3. pa	A.4. di
B.1. nü	B.2. re	B.3. chi	B.4. zhu
C.1. mo	C.2. qu	C.3. ca	C.4. si
D.1. tu	D.2. fo	D.3. ze	D.4. ju
E.1. lü	E.2. bu	E.3. xi	E.4. shi
F.1. gu	F.2. se	F.3. ci	F.4. ku
G.1. mang	G.2. quan	G.3. yuan	G.4. yue
H.1. yi	H.2. er	H.3. san	H.4. si

I.1. ba   I.2. qi   I.3. liu   I.4. wu

J.1. jiu   J.2. shi   J.3. tian   J.4. jin

K.1. mu   K.2. shui   K.3. huo   K.4. ren

L.1. yu   L.2. zhuang   L.3. qun   L.4. zhong

III. Compound Finals:

A. Please fill in the blanks with compound finals.

1.a. zh_____   1.b. t_____   1.c. k_____   1.d. j_____

2.a. x_____   2.b. q_____   2.c. j_____   2.d. d_____

3.a. x_____   3.b. zh_____   3.c. t_____   3.d. g_____

4.a. sh_____   4.b. b_____   4.c. z_____   4.d. q_____

5.a. j_____   5.b. d_____   5.c. x_____   5.d. ch_____

6.a. zh_____   6.b. l_____   6.c. k_____   6.d. j_____

7.a. s_____   7.b. x_____   7.c. p_____   7.d. ch_____

B. Please fill in the blanks with compound finals and mark appropriate tone marks.

1.a. m_____   1.b. zh_____   1.c. sh_____   1.d. zh_____

2.a. sh_____   2.b. t_____   2.c. l_____   2.d. b_____

3.a. s_____   3.b. j_____   3.c. k_____   3.d. d_____

4.a. l_____   4.b. q_____   4.c. t_____   4.d. x_____

5.a. f_____   5.b. p_____   5.c. x_____   5.d. j_____

6.a. b_____   6.b. j_____   6.c. q_____   6.d. t_____

7.a. l_____   7.b. g_____   7.c. q_____   7.d. x_____

IV. Neutral Tones:

Please listen to the tape and mark the tone marks.

A.1. guanxi	A.2. kuzi	A.3. shifu	A.4. keqi
B.1. zhuozi	B.2. gaosu	B.3. shufu	B.4. women
C.1. gege	C.2. weizi	C.3. dongxi	C.4. yisi
D.1. nimen	D.2. shihou	D.3. chuqu	D.4. pengyou
E.1. meimei	E.2. xihuan	E.3. jiaozi	E.4. xiansheng
F.1. zenme	F.2. didi	F.3. erzi	F.4. xiexie
G.1. jiejie	G.2. mafan	G.3. bobo	G.4. yizi

V. Exercises for Initials, Finals, and Tones: Monosyllablic Words

Please transcribe what you hear into *pinyin* with tone marks.

A.1. _____	A.2. _____	A.3. _____	A.4. _____
B.1. _____	B.2. _____	B.3. _____	B.4. _____
C.1. _____	C.2. _____	C.3. _____	C.4. _____
D.1. _____	D.2. _____	D.3. _____	D.4. _____
E.1. _____	E.2. _____	E.3. _____	E.4. _____
F.1. _____	F.2. _____	F.3. _____	F.4. _____
G.1. _____	G.2. _____	G.3. _____	G.4. _____
H.1. _____	H.2. _____	H.3. _____	H.4. _____
I.1. _____	I.2. _____	I.3. _____	I.4. _____

VI. Exercises for Initials, Finals, and Tones: Bisyllabic Words

Please transcribe what you hear into *pinyin* with correct tone marks.

A.1. _____   A.2. _____   A.3. _____   A.4. _____

B.1. _____   B.2. _____   B.3. _____   B.4. _____

C.1. _____   C.2. _____   C.3. _____   C.4. _____

D.1. _____   D.2. _____   D.3. _____   D.4. _____

E.1. _____   E.2. _____   E.3. _____   E.4. _____

F.1. _____   F.2. _____   F.3. _____   F.4. _____

VII. Exercises for Initials, Finals, and Tones: Cities

Please read the following words and identify which cities they are.

Example: Mài'āmì   ---> <u>Miami</u>

1. Bōshìdùn   --->   _____

2. Lúndūn   --->   _____

3. Niǔyuē   --->   _____

4. Bālí   --->   _____

5. Zhījiāgē   --->   _____

6. Běijīng   --->   _____

7. Luòshānjī   --->   _____

8. Duōlúnduō   --->   _____

9. Xīyǎtú   --->   _____

10. Wēinísī   --->   _____

VIII. Exercises for Initials, Finals, and Tones: Celebrities
Please read the following words and identify which celebrities they are.

1. Mǎdānnà   ---> _____

2. Màikè Jiékèsēn   ---> _____

3. Yīlìshābái Tàilè   ---> _____

4. Bābālā Sīcuìshān   ---> _____

5. Aòdàilì Hèběn   ---> _____

6. Suǒfēiyǎ Luólán   ---> _____

7. Mǎlìlián Mènglù   ---> _____

IX. Exercises for Initials, Finals, and Tones: Countries
Please transcribe what you hear into *pinyin* with tone marks and identify what countries they are.

Example: <u>Rìběn</u>   --->   <u>Japan</u>

1. _____ ---> _____

2. _____ ---> _____

3. _____ ---> _____

4. _____ ---> _____

5. _____ ---> _____

6. _____ ---> _____

7. _____ ---> _____

8. _____ ---> _____

9. _____ ---> _____

10. _____ ---> _____

X. Exercises for Initials, Finals, and Tones: American Presidents

Please transcribe what you hear into *pinyin* with tone marks and identify which Amercian presidents they are.

1. _____ ---> _____

2. _____ ---> _____

3. _____ ---> _____

4. _____ ---> _____

5. _____ ---> _____

6. _____ ---> _____

7. _____ ---> _____

8. _____ ---> _____

9. _____ ---> _____

10. _____ ---> _____

Lesson One   Greetings

I. LISTENING COMPREHENSION

Section One (Listen to the tape for the textbook)

A. Dialogue I (Multiple choice)

(   ) 1. What did the man say to the woman?
    a. What's your name?
    b. I'm Mr. Wang.
    c. Are you Miss Li?
    d. How do you do!

(   ) 2. What is the woman's name?
    a. Wang Peng
    b. Li You
    c. Xing Li
    d. Jiao Li You

(   ) 3. What is the man's name?
    a. Wang Peng
    b. Li You
    c. Xing Wang
    d. Jiao Wang Peng

B. Dialogue II (True/ False)

(   ) 1. Miss Li is a student.
(   ) 2. Mr. Wang is a teacher.
(   ) 3. Mr. Wang is an American.
(   ) 4. Miss Li is a Chinese.

Section Two (Listen to the tape for the workbook) (Multiple choice)

A. Dialogue I

(   ) These two people are _____.
    a. saying good-bye to each other
    b. asking each other's name
    c. greeting each other
    d. asking each other's nationality

B. Dialogue II

(   ) 1. The two speakers are most likely _____.
    a. brother and sister
    b. father and daughter
    c. old friends reuniting
    d. strangers getting acquainted

(   ) 2. Who are these two people? They are _____.
    a. Mr. Li and Miss You
    b. Mr. Li and Miss Li

    c. Mr. Wang and Miss You

    d. Mr. Wang and Miss Wang

C. Dialogue III

(   ) Which of the following is true?

    a. Both the man and the woman are Chinese.

    b. Both the man and the woman are American.

    c. The man is Chinese and the woman is American.

    d. The man is American and the woman is Chinese.

D. Dialogue IV

(   ) Which of the following is true?

    a. Both the man and the woman are teachers.

    b. Both the man and the woman are students.

    c. The man is a teacher and the woman is a student.

    d. The man is a student and the woman is a teacher.

II. SPEAKING EXERCISES

Section One (Answer the following questions in Chinese based on the dialogues)
A. Dialogue I

    1. How does Mr. Wang greet Miss Li in Chinese?

    2. What does Miss Li reply?

    3. How does Mr. Wang ask what Miss Li's surname is?

    4. What is Mr. Wang's given name?

    5. How does Mr. Wang ask what Miss Li's given name is?

    6. What is Miss Li's given name?

B. Dialogue II

    1. How does Miss Li ask whether Mr. Wang is a teacher or not?

    2. Is Mr. Wang a teacher?

    3. Is Miss Li a teacher?

    4. What is Mr. Wang's nationality?

    5. What is Miss Li's nationality?

Section Two
A. You meet a middle-aged Chinese person on campus. Try to ask politely in Chinese whether he/she is a teacher.

B. You meet a Chinese student on campus:

    1. Greet him/her in Chinese.

    2. Ask his/her name.

C. Introduce yourself in Chinese to a Chinese student. Tell him/her what your name is and whether you are a student.

D. You just met a foreign student who can speak Chinese.

    1. Ask him/her whether he/she is Chinese.

    2. Tell him/her that you are American.

III. READING COMPREHENSION

Section One

A. Give *pinyin* for the following Chinese phrases:

1. 你好_____   2. 貴姓 _____   3. 名字 _____

4. 小姐 _____   5. 老師 _____   6. 中國人 _____

7. 學生 _____   8. 先生 _____   9. 美國人 _____

B. Match the questions on the left side with the appropriate replies on the right. Write down the letter in the parentheses.

( ) 1. 你好！   A. 是,我是老師。

( ) 2. 您貴姓？   B. 不,我是中國人。

( ) 3. 你是美國人嗎？   C. 我也是學生。

( ) 4. 你是老師嗎？   D. 我姓李。

( ) 5. 我是學生，你呢？   E. 你好！

C. Read the passage and answer the questions. (True/False)

王小姐是中國學生。李先生是美國老師。

( ) 1. 王小姐姓王。

( ) 2. 王小姐是美國人。

( ) 3. 王小姐不是老師。

( ) 4. 李先生不是中國人。

( ) 5. 李先生是老師。

Section Two

Chinese Business Cards

Below are four real Chinese business cards. Circle all of the characters that you recognize, and underline the characters denoting family names.

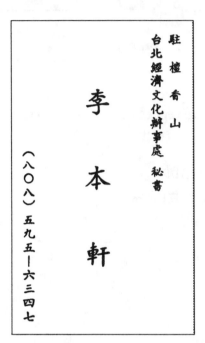

駐檀香山
台北經濟文化辦事處　秘書

李本軒

（八〇八）五九五—六三四七

美國夏威夷大學東亞語文系教授

李英哲
YINGCHE LI

EAST ASIAN LANGUAGES AND LITERATURES
UNIVERSITY OF HAWAII
HONOLULU, HAWAII 96822
U.S.A

TEL : (808) 956-8406 (O)
FAX: (808) 956-9515
INTERNET : yli@ssc.lang.hawaii.edu

台北美國學校
外語系中文部主任

王智寧

校址：台北市士林區中山北路六段114巷6號二四〇
傳真電話：八七三一九九〇〇
住宅電話：台北市中山北路七段57巷二四八〇
電話／傳真：（〇二）八七一一一四六九樓一三

中外合資
常州華潤裝飾工程有限公司
CHANGZHOU HUA RUN DECORATION ENGINEERING CO. LTD

王德中
WANG DE ZHONG
首席　副總经理

地址：中國常州勞動中路 42 號
ADD:№42 LAO DONG RD(M) CHANGZHOU
電話 TEL:8824743　8813361
傳真 FAX:0519－8824743
電挂 CABLE:5000　郵編 P C:213001
宅電 HOME:6622599

IV. Writing & Grammar Exercises

Section One

A. Give the Chinese characters for the following sentences that are in *pinyin*.

1. Nín guì xìng?

2. Nǐ jiào shénme míngzi?

3. Qǐng wèn, nǐ shì xuésheng ma?

4. Wǒ shì Zhōngguórén. Nǐ ne?

5. Wǒ bú xìng Wáng, wǒ xìng Lǐ.

6. Nín shì lǎoshī, wǒ shì xuésheng.

7. Nǐ shì Měiguórén, wǒ yě shì Měiguórén.

B. Rearrange the given Chinese words into a sentence, using the English sentence as a clue.

1. 叫 / 名字 / 你 / 請問 / 什麼
   (May I ask what your name is?)

2. 姓 / 王 / 嗎 / 你
   (Is your surname Wang?)

3. 嗎 / 是 / 你 / 學生 / 美國
   (Are you an American student?)

4. 中國 / 是 / 人 / 我 / 不
   (I am not Chinese.)

5. 小姐 / 先生 / 美國人 / 美國人 / 王 / 李 / 也 / 是 / 是
   (Miss Li is American. Mr. Wang is also American.)

C. Change the following statements into questions.

Example: 我是學生。 ===> 你是學生嗎？

1. 我是美國人。

2. 我姓李。

3. 王老師是中國人。

4. 李小姐不是學生。

5. 我也是學生。

D. Answer the following questions in Chinese.

1. 您貴姓？

2. 你叫什麼名字？

3. 你是學生嗎？

4. 李小姐是美國人。你呢？

5. 王先生是中國學生。你呢？

E. In each group, use 也 to connect the two sentences into a compound sentence.

Example: 李友是學生。/ 王朋是學生。

===> 李友是學生，王朋也是學生。

1. 你是美國人。/ 我是美國人。

2. 李小姐不是中國人。/ 李先生不是中國人。

3. 你不姓王。/ 我不姓王。

4. 王先生是老師。/ 李小姐是老師。

F. Translate the following sentences by using the Chinese words or phrases given in
    parentheses .

    1. I am American. (是)

    2. Are you Chinese? (是，嗎)

    3. May I ask what your surname is? (請問，貴姓)

    4. My surname is Li. My name is Li You. (我姓..., 我叫...)

    5. I am a teacher. How about you? (呢)

    6. *A:* I am an American student. Are you an American student, too? (也)

       B: No, I am a Chinese student. (不)

Section Two

A. Write your Chinese name in characters if you have one.

B. Without looking at the book, write as many characters as you can from Lesson One.

Lesson Two   Family

I. LISTENING COMPREHENSION

Section One (Listen to the tape for the textbook)

A. Dialogue I (True/False)
(   ) 1. The picture in question belongs to Wang Peng.
(   ) 2. Little Gao doesn't have any younger brothers.
(   ) 3. Little Gao's parents are in the picture.
(   ) 4. All the people in the picture are members of Little Gao's family.
(   ) 5. Mr. Li does not have any sons.

B. Dialogue II (Multiple choice)
(   ) 1. How many people are there in Little Zhang's family?
     a. 3   b. 4   c. 5   d. 6

(   ) 2. How many people are there in Li You's family?
     a. 3   b. 4   c. 5   d. 6

(   ) 3. How many older sisters does Little Zhang have?
     a. 0   b. 1   c. 2   d. 3

(   ) 4. How many younger sisters does Li You have?
     a. 0   b. 1   c. 2   d. 3

(   ) 5. How many older brothers does Little Zhang have?
     a. 0   b. 1   c. 2   d. 3

(   ) 6. How many younger brothers does Little Zhang have?
     a. 0   b. 1   c. 2   d. 3

(   ) 7. How many children do Little Zhang's parents have?
     a. 2   b. 3   c. 4   d. 5

(   ) 8. How many sons do Li You's parents have?
     a. 0   b. 1   c. 2   d. 3

(   ) 9. Little Zhang's father is a _____.
     a. lawyer   b. teacher   c. doctor   d. student

(   ) 10. Li You's mother is a _____.
     a. lawyer   b. teacher   c. doctor   d. student

Section Two (Listen to the tape for the workbook) (Multiple choice)

A. Dialogue I
(   ) Who are the people in the picture?
      a. The woman's father and mother.
      b. The woman's mother and younger sister.
      c. The woman's older sister and younger sister.
      d. The woman's mother and older sister.

B. Dialogue II
(   ) 1. Which of the following is true?
      a. Both the man and the woman have older brothers.
      b. Both the man and the woman have younger brothers.
      c. The man has an older brother but no younger brother.
      d. The man has a younger brother but no older brother.

(   ) 2. Why does the woman laugh at the end of the conversation? Because she finds it
      funny that _____.
      a. neither the man nor she herself has younger brothers
      b. neither the man nor she herself has older brothers
      c. the man has failed to count himself as his older brother's younger brother
      d. the man has failed to count himself as his younger brother's older brother

C. Dialogue III
(   ) 1. The man's mother is a _____.
      a. teacher   b. student   c. doctor   d. lawyer

(   ) 2. The woman's father is a _____.
      a. teacher   b. student   c. doctor   d. lawyer

D. Dialogue IV
(   ) 1. How many brothers does the woman have?
      a. 1   b. 2   c. 3   d. 4

(   ) 2. How many daughters do the woman's parents have?
      a. 1   b. 2   c. 3   d. 4

(   ) 3. How many people in the woman's family are older than herself?
      a. 2   b. 3   c. 4   d. 5

(   ) 4. How many people in the man's family are younger than himself?
      a. 0   b. 1   c. 2   d. 3

(   ) 5. Why do the speakers disagree on the number of the people in the man's family?
      Because he forgot to count in _____.
      a. his older brother   b. his younger sister
      c. his younger brother   d. himself

II. SPEAKING EXERCISES

Section One (Answer the following questions in Chinese based on the dialogues)
A. Dialogue I
1. Whose photo is on the wall?
2. How many people are there in Little Gao's family? Who are they?
3. Is the boy in the picture Little Gao's younger brother? How do you know?
4. Is the girl in the picture Little Gao's younger sister? How do you know?

B. Dialogue II
1. How many people are there in Little Zhang's family?
2. How many children do Little Zhang's parents have?
3. What is the birth order of Little Zhang?
4. How many brothers and sisters does Li You have?
5. What is the occupation of Little Zhang's father?
6. What is the occupation of Little Zhang's mother and Li You's mother?
7. How many people are there in Li You's family?
8. How many daughters do Li You's parents have?

Section Two

A. Find a family picture and use this to introduce your family members to your friends.

B. Show your family photo to your partner and ask questions about each other's photo, such as: who the person is, if your partner has brothers or sisters, what each of his/her family members does.

C. Following are four members from Wang You's family. Please introduce them. Make sure that you mention what they do.
   1. Wang You's older brother.
   2. Wang You's mother.
   3. Wang You's father.
   4. Wang You's younger brother.

D. Introduce the family in the picture below. Please use as many new words as possible from this lesson.

III. READING COMPREHENSION

Section One

A. Match the questions on the left with the appropriate replies on the right. Write down the letter in the parentheses.

(　)1.這個人是誰？　　　　　*A.* 是我的。

(　)2.這張照片是誰的？　　　*B.* 這是我姐姐。

(　)3.你哥哥是學生嗎？　　　*C.* 我家有五個人。

(　)4.你家有幾個人？　　　　*D.* 我有兩個弟弟。

(　)5.你有沒有弟弟？　　　　*E.* 我哥哥是醫生。

B. This is a family portrait of the Gao family. Look at the photo carefully and identify each person.

1. 爸爸 (　)　　2. 妹妹 (　)　　3. 媽媽 (　)　　4. 姐姐 (　)

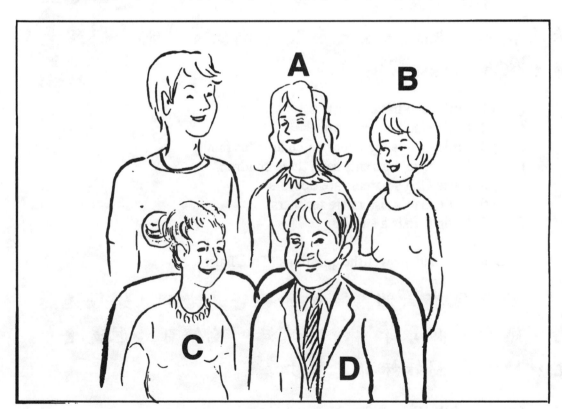

C. Give *pinyin* for the following Chinese words, and draw lines to connect the Chinese words and their English equivalents.

1. 爸爸   mother

2. 哥哥   younger sister

3. 弟弟   older sister

4. 妹妹   older brother

5. 媽媽   younger brother

6. 姐姐   father

7. 誰   how many

8. 幾   who

9. 誰的   whose

Section Two

A. Read the passage and answer the questions (True/False)

小高家有五個人，爸爸、媽媽、一個姐姐、一個妹妹和他。他的爸爸是醫生，媽媽是律師，姐姐是老師，他和妹妹都是學生。

(   ) 1. Little Gao has two sisters.

(   ) 2. Little Gao has one brother.

(   ) 3. Little Gao is the youngest child in his family.

(   ) 4. Little Gao's parents have three children.

(   ) 5. Little Gao's parents are doctors.

(   ) 6. Little Gao's sisters are teachers.

(   ) 7. Little Gao is a student.

B. Read the passage and answer the questions (True/False)

小王家有六個人。她的爸爸是老師，媽媽是醫生。她有一個哥哥、兩個妹妹。她的哥哥也是醫生，她和兩個妹妹都是學生。

(   ) 1. Little Wang is the oldest child in the family.

(   ) 2. Little Wang's father and her brother are both teachers.

(   ) 3. Little Wang's parents have only one son.

(   ) 4. Little Wang's mother and brother are both doctors.

(   ) 5. All the girls in the Wang family are students.

IV. WRITING & GRAMMAR EXERCISES

Section One

A. Answer the following questions about yourself in complete sentences, using 有 or 沒有. If the answer is positive, please state how many there are.

      Examples: 1. *A:* 你有哥哥嗎？   *B:* 我沒有哥哥。

            2. *A:* 你有哥哥嗎？   *B:* 我有三個哥哥。

1. *A:* 你有姐姐嗎？   *B:* _____。

2. *A:* 你有妹妹嗎？   *B:* _____。

3. *A:* 你有弟弟嗎？   *B:* _____。

4. *A:* 你有哥哥嗎？   *B:* _____。

B. Rewrite the following sentences using 都

    Example: 小高是學生，王朋也是學生。

        ===>小高、王朋都是學生。

1. 小高有姐姐，小張也有姐姐。

2. 王朋是學生，李友也是學生。

3. 這張照片是你的，那張照片也是你的。

4. 這個人姓李，那個人也姓李。

5. 李友沒有我的照片，王朋也沒有我的照片。

6. 他哥哥不是律師，他弟弟也不是律師。

7. 王朋有哥哥，小高有哥哥，李友沒有哥哥。

8. 我爸爸是醫生，我媽媽是醫生，我哥哥是律師。

C. Fill in the blanks with "這" or "那" based on the descriptions for each situation.

1. You point to a person standing about thirty feet away, and say:

　　_____個人是我的老師，他是中國人。

2. You are holding a family photo in your hand, and say:

　　_____是我爸爸，_____是我媽媽。

3. You look down the hallway and recognize someone, and say:

　　_____個醫生叫李生一，是李友的爸爸。

4. You introduce to your friend a girl sitting at the same table, and say:

　　_____是李先生的女兒。

D. Fill in the blanks with the appropriate question words. (什麼、誰、誰的、幾)

1. *A:* _____名字叫王朋？   *B:* 他的名字叫王朋。

2. *A:* 李老師家有_____個人？   *B:* 他家有三個人。

3. *A:* 你爸爸做_____？   *B:* 我爸爸是醫生。

4. *A:* 你妹妹叫_____名字？   *B:* 我妹妹叫高美美。

5. *A:* 那個美國人是_____？   *B:* 他叫 David Smith，是我的老師。

6. *A:* 你有_____張你媽媽的照片？   *B:* 我有兩張。

E. Translate the following sentences into Chinese, using the words and phrases given in parentheses.

1. Little Wang, is this photograph yours? （ 是⋯嗎？ ）

2. Mr. Zhang has three daughters.

3. Mr. Wang has no sons.

4. Is this boy your older brother?

5. Is this girl your younger sister?

6. *A:* Who is this person? （ 誰 ）

   B: She's my younger sister. （是）

7. *A:* Is that your older brother?

   B: No, he's my father. （ 不是 ）

8. *A:* Do you have any younger brothers? （有）

B: No, I don't have any younger brothers. （没有）

9. *A:* How many older sisters do you have? （有，幾）

   B: I have two older sisters.

10. How many people are there in your family? （有，幾）

11. There are six people in my family: my dad, my mom, two older brothers, a younger sister and I. （有）

12. *A:* What do your older brothers and older sisters do? （什麼）

    B: My older brothers and older sisters are all students.

13. *A:* My mom is a lawyer. My dad is a doctor. How about your mom and dad? （呢）

    B: My mom is a lawyer, too. My dad is a teacher. （也）

14. Both my teacher and her teacher are Americans.

15. Neither Little Gao nor Little Zhang is Chinese.

Section Two

A. List your family members in Chinese.

B. To the best of your Chinese ability, tell what each of your family members does.

C. Please write a paragraph describing the picture below?

Some suggestions:

This is Little Zhang's picture. Little Zhang is my friend. He is Chinese.
He is a teacher. He has seven students

Lesson Three   Dates and Time

I. LISTENING COMPREHENSION

Section One (Listen to the tape for the textbook) (True/False)

A. Dialogue I

(   ) 1. Little Gao is eighteen years old.
(   ) 2. September 12 is Thursday.
(   ) 3. October 7 is Little Gao's birthday.
(   ) 4. Little Bai will treat Little Gao to a dinner on Thursday.
(   ) 5. Little Gao is American; therefore he likes American food.
(   ) 6. Little Bai refuses to eat American food.
(   ) 7. They will have dinner together at 6:30.

B. Dialogue II

(   ) 1. Wang Peng will not be free until 6:15.
(   ) 2. Wang Peng will not be busy tomorrow.
(   ) 3. Little Bai is inviting Wang Peng to dinner.
(   ) 4. Tomorrow is Little Bai's birthday.
(   ) 5. Wang Peng doesn't know Little Gao.
(   ) 6. Little Li is Little Bai's schoolmate.
(   ) 7. Wang Peng doesn't know Little Li.

Section Two (Listen to the tape for the workbook)

A. Dialogue I (Multiple choice)

(   ) 1. Today's date is _____.
          a. May 10   b. June 10   c. October 5   d. October 6

(   ) 2. What day is today?
          a. Thursday   b. Friday   c. Saturday   d. Sunday

(   ) 3. What day is October 7? It is _____.
          a. Thursday   b. Friday   c. Saturday   d. Sunday

B. Dialogue II (True/False)

(   ) 1. Both speakers in the dialogue are Chinese.
(   ) 2. The man invites the woman to dinner because it will be his birthday tomorrow.
(   ) 3. The man likes Chinese food.
(   ) 4. The woman does not like Chinese food.

C. Dialogue III (True/False)

(   ) 1. Today the woman is busy.
(   ) 2. Today the man is not busy.
(   ) 3. Tomorrow both the man and the woman will be very busy.

33

D. Dialogue IV (Multiple choice)

(   ) 1. What time does the man propose to meet?
        a. 6:30   b. 7:00   c. 7:30   d. 8:00

(   ) 2. What time do they finally agree upon?
        a. 6:30   b. 7:00   c. 7:30   d. 8:00

(   ) 3. What day are they going to meet?
        a. Thursday
        b. Friday
        c. Saturday
        d. Sunday

II. SPEAKING EXERCISES

Section One (Answer the following questions in Chinese based on the dialogues)

A. Dialogue I
1. When is Little Gao's birthday?
2. How old is Little Gao?
3. Who is going to treat whom?
4. What is Little Gao's nationality?
5. What kind of dinner are they going to have?
6. What time is the dinner?

B. Dialogue II
1. Why does Little Bai ask if Wang Peng is busy or not?
2. When is Wang Peng busy?
3. Who else will go out for dinner tomorrow with Little Bai and Wang Peng?
4. Does Little Bai know Little Li? How do you know?

Section Two

A. Tomorrow is your partner's birthday. Find out how old he/she is and offer to take him/her out for dinner. Ask him/her if he/she prefers Chinese or American food and decide the time for the dinner.

B. Invite a mutual friend to join you and your partner for the dinner. Explain what the occasion is and who else will be there.

C. Your partner would like to take you out for dinner on your birthday, but you will be very busy on your birthday. Suggest another day for the dinner and decide the time for the dinner.

III. READING COMPREHENSION

Section One

A. Read the passages and answer the questions. (Multiple choice)

(   ) 1. 今天星期六，明天星期幾？
   a. Thursday
   b. Friday
   c. Saturday
   d. Sunday

(   ) 2. 十月二號星期四，十月四號星期幾？
   a. 星期四
   b. 星期五
   c. 星期六
   d. 星期日

B. Write the following times in English.

   1. 三點鐘：_____

   2. 兩點十分：_____

   3. 六點五十分：_____

   4. 晚上八點鐘：_____

   5. 晚上九點一刻：_____

   6. 晚上十一點半：_____

C. Fill in the blanks in English below based on the calendar.

1997 年	The date on this calendar is _____.
九　月	The day of the week is _____.
22日	Next month is _____.
星期一	The day after tomorrow is a _____.

Section Two

A. Read the passage and answer the questions. (True/False)

明天是小白的同學小高的生日。小白和他姐姐請
小高吃飯，因為小白的姐姐也認識小高。小高是美國
人，可是他喜歡吃中國飯。明天晚上他們吃中國飯。

(   ) 1. Tomorrow is Little Bai's birthday.
(   ) 2. Little Bai's sister knows Little Gao.
(   ) 3. Little Gao and Little Bai are classmates.
(   ) 4. Little Gao is Chinese.
(   ) 5. Little Gao likes Chinese food.
(   ) 6. Little Gao is going to pay for the dinner.

B. Read the passage and answer the questions. (True/False)

李小姐、白小姐和高先生是同學。今天是李小姐的
生日，晚上六點半白小姐和高先生的妹妹請她吃晚
飯，可是李小姐不認識高先生的妹妹。

(   ) 1. Miss Li and Miss Bai are classmates.
(   ) 2. Miss Li is going to treat Miss Bai to dinner tonight.
(   ) 3. Today is Miss Li's birthday.
(   ) 4. Miss Li will not have dinner at home this evening.
(   ) 5. Miss Li will see Mr. Gao at 6: 30 p. m..
(   ) 6. Miss Li and Mr. Gao's younger sister are close friends.

C. Which of the following is the correct way to say "June 3, 1997" in Chinese?

1. 六月三日一九九七年

2. 三日六月一九九七年

3. 六月一九九七年三日

4. 一九九七年六月三日

The correct answer is: _____ .

IV. WRITING & GRAMMAR EXERCISES

Section One

A. Write the following numbers using Chinese characters.

1. 15 _____

2. 93 _____

3. 47 _____

4. 62 _____

5. your phone number _____

B. Turn the following dates or time phrases into Chinese and write down the Chinese version in characters.

1. November 12 _____

2. Friday evening _____

3. 7:00 this evening _____

4. 8:30 p.m. Saturday _____

5. quarter after nine _____

C. Please complete the following exchanges.

1. *A:* 今天是幾月幾號？　　　　　*B:* _____。

2. *A:* 你的生日是_____？　　*B:* 我的生日是_____。

3. *A:* 你今年多大？　　　　　　　*B:* _____。

4. *A:* 現在幾點鐘？　　　　　　　*B:* 現在_____點_____分。

5. *A:* _____？　*B:* 我五點三刻吃晚飯。

D. Please complete the following questions using "A-not-A" form.
　　　Example: *A:* 王朋明天有沒有事？
　　　　　　　　B: 王朋明天沒有事。

1. *A:* _____?

   B: 王先生是中國人。

2. *A:* _____?

   B: 小高沒有弟弟。

3. *A:* _____?

   B: 小高喜歡吃美國飯。

4. *A:* _____?

   B: 王朋明天不忙。

5. *A:* _____?

   B: 小張的爸爸不是醫生。

E. Please complete the following questions with 還是
    Example: *A:* 王朋是中國人還是美國人？
             B: 王朋是中國人。

1. *A:* _____?

   B: 我喜歡吃美國飯。

2. *A:* _____?

   B: 小白是小高的同學。

3. *A:* _____?

   B: 小張的爸爸是律師。

4. *A:* _____?

   B: 李友不是老師。

5. *A:* _____?

   B: 星期二是我的生日。

F. Based on the text, please answer the following questions with 因爲.

1. 小白爲什麼請小高吃飯？

2. 小白爲什麼不請小高吃中國飯？

3. 小白爲什麼問王朋忙不忙？

4. 小白爲什麼認識小李？

G. Rearrange the following Chinese words into sentences, using the given English sentences as clues.

1. 我 / 吃飯 / 今天 / 你 / 怎麼樣 / 晚上 / 請
   How does it sound if I take you out for dinner this evening?

2. 星期四 / 星期五 / 吃飯 / 我 / 你 / 還是 / 請 / 請 / 吃飯 / 我
   Is it Thursday or Friday that you are going to take me out for dinner?

3. 哥哥 / 小張 / 認識 / 他的 / 我 / 我 / 可是 / 不 / 認識
   I do not know Little Zhang, but I know his brother.

4. 美國人 / 美國飯 / 可是 / 他 / 不 / 喜歡 / 吃 / 是 / 他
   He is American, but he does not like American food.

H. Translate the following sentences into Chinese, using the words and phrases given in parentheses:

1. What day of the week is June 3? （幾）

2. Whose birthday is August 7? （誰的）

3. What month and day is your dad's birthday? （幾）

4. How old is Little Gao (this year)? （多大）

5. Is Wang Peng Chinese or American? （還是）

6. Little Bai is American, but he likes Chinese food. （可是）

7. Who will you invite to dinner on Monday evening? （誰）

8. *A:* When are we having dinner tomorrow evening? （幾點鐘）

   B: Half past seven.

9. Little Zhang, will you be busy Thursday evening? （V 不 V）

10. We will treat our classmates to dinner, how is that? （怎麼樣）

11. *A:* Why are you busy today? （爲什麼，因爲）

    B: Because today is my mom's birthday.

12. I know my older brother's classmate, Little Zhang.

Section Two

A. Write today's date in Chinese.

B. Write the currect time in Chinese.

C. Write a note to your friend inviting him/her to have dinner with you tomorrow because it's your birthday.

D. Write a paragraph describing the picture below.

You must mention:

1. The date
2. The time
3. The occasion
4. Who are present

Lesson Four   Hobbies

I. LISTENING COMPREHENSION

Section One (Listen to the tape for the textbook) (True/False)

A. Dialogue I
(   ) 1. Little Gao likes watching T.V.
(   ) 2. Little Bai does a lot of reading every weekend.
(   ) 3. Little Bai likes not only singing, but also dancing.
(   ) 4. Little Gao likes playing ball and listening to music on weekends.
(   ) 5. Both Little Gao and Little Bai like dancing.
(   ) 6. Little Bai is treating Little Gao to a movie.

B. Dialogue II
(   ) 1. Little Zhang does not like playing ball.
(   ) 2. Wang Peng wants to play ball this weekend.
(   ) 3. Little Zhang is very interested in movies.
(   ) 4. Wang Peng is going out to eat with Little Zhang.
(   ) 5. Little Zhang likes to sleep.
(   ) 6. In the end Wang Peng gives up the idea of going out with Little Zhang.

Section Two (Listen to the tape for the workbook)

Dialogue I (Multiple choice)
(   ) 1. What will the man most likely do on weekends?
　　　　　a. go to concert　　　　b. play ball
　　　　　c. go to the movies　　　d. go dancing

(   ) 2. If the man and the woman decide to do something together over the weekend,
　　　　　they will most likely go to _____.
　　　　　a. a movie　　b. a concert　　c. a dance　　d. a ball game

Dialogue II (True/False)
(   ) 1. The woman doesn't like Chinese movies because her Chinese is not good
　　　　　enough.
(   ) 2. The woman prefers American movies over Chinese movies.
(   ) 3. The man invites the woman to an American movie at the end of the
　　　　　conversation.

Dialogue III (True/False)
(   ) 1. The woman invites the man to a concert.
(   ) 2. The man is interested in sports.
(   ) 3. The man invites the woman to go dancing.

Dialogue IV (Multiple choice)

(   ) 1. The man invites the woman to _____.
      a. a dinner   b. a movie
      c. a dance   d. a concert

(   ) 2. The man gives the invitation because _____.
      a. the woman has invited him to a dinner before
      b. the woman has invited him to a concert before
      c. tomorrow is his birthday
      d. tomorrow is her birthday

(   ) 3. Which of the following statements is true?
      a. The woman doesn't accept the invitation although she will not be busy tomorrow.
      b. The woman doesn't accept the invitation because she'll be busy tomorrow.
      c. The woman accepts the invitation although she'll be busy tomorrow.
      d. The woman accepts the invitation because she will not be busy tomorrow.

E. Narrative (Multiple choice)

(   ) 1. The speaker probably spends most of his spare time _____.
      a. in movie theaters   b. in concert halls
      c. in front of a TV set   d. in a library

(   ) 2. According to the speaker, Wang Peng loves _____.
      a. movies and TV   b. dancing and books
      c. dancing and music   d. books only

(   ) 3. Which of the following statements is true about the speaker and Wang Peng?
      a. Wang Peng likes to read.
      b. The speaker likes to watch TV.
      c. Both the speaker and Wang Peng like to dance.
      d. Wang Peng and the speaker are classmates.

Which one on the left side is known as "dǎqiú" in Chinese?

II. SPEAKING EXERCISES

Section One (Answer the following questions in Chinese based on the dialogues)
A. Dialogue I
> 1. What does Little Gao like to do on weekends?
> 2. What does Little Bai like to do on weekends?
> 3. What will Little Bai and Little Gao do tonight?
> 4. Who is treating tonight?
> 5. Who took whom to dinner yesterday?

B. Dialogue II
> 1. Did Wang Peng see Little Zhang yesterday? How do you know?
> 2. Does Little Zhang want to play ball? Why?
> 3. Does Little Zhang want to go to the movies? Why?
> 4. What does Little Zhang like to do?
> 5. What did Wang Peng finally decide to do this weekend?

Section Two
A. Discuss your interests and hobbies with your friends, and then make an appointment with them based on your common interest.

B. Your partner is inviting you to do something. Keep rejecting the suggestions he/she gives and give reasons why you do not like those activities.

C. How do you say the following sports in Chinese?

III. READING COMPREHENSION

Section One

A. Match the phrases with the appropriate pictures.

( ) 1. 打球 ( ) 2. 跳舞 ( ) 3. 唱歌 ( ) 4. 聽音樂 ( ) 5. 看電視

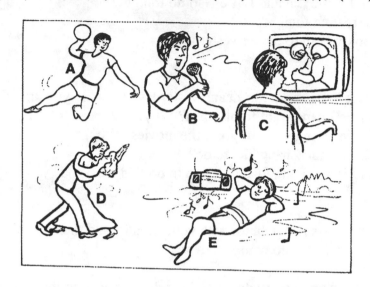

B. Match the questions on the left with the appropriate replies on the right. Write down the letter in the parentheses.

( ) 1. 你叫什麼名字？　　　　　A. 我明天不忙。
( ) 2. 這是你弟弟嗎？　　　　　B. 今天晚上我很忙。
( ) 3. 你明天忙不忙？　　　　　C. 我想看一個外國電影。
( ) 4. 你認識小張嗎？　　　　　D. 不,這是我哥哥。
( ) 5. 你喜歡聽音樂嗎？　　　　E. 因爲我喜歡吃美國飯。
( ) 6. 爲什麼你請我看電影？　　F. 認識,他是我同學。
( ) 7. 爲什麼我們不吃中國飯？　G. 我叫王朋。
( ) 8. 我們去打球,好嗎？　　　H. 我覺得聽音樂沒有意思。
( ) 9. 這個週末你做什麼？　　　I. 我不想打球。
( ) 10. 今天晚上我去找你,好嗎？　J. 因爲今天是你的生日。

Section Two

A. Read the passage and answer the questions. (True/False)

昨天是張律師的生日，他的同學王先生昨天晚上請他吃晚飯。因爲王先生請張律師吃飯，所以張律師這個週末想請王先生去看一個外國電影。

(　　) 1. Yesterday was Lawyer Wang's birthday.
(　　) 2. Yesterday Lawyer Zhang didn't have dinner at home.
(　　) 3. Yesterday Mr. Wang and Lawyer Zhang went to see a foreign movie.
(　　) 4. Mr. Wang wants to take Lawyer Zhang to see a movie because Lawyer Zhang took him out for dinner.

B. Read the passage and answer the questions. (Multiple choice)

小王和小李是同學。小王是中國人，他喜歡打球、看電視和看書。小李是美國人，她喜歡聽音樂、唱歌和跳舞。他們都喜歡看電影，可是小王只喜歡看美國電影，小李覺得美國電影沒有什麼意思，她只喜歡看外國電影。她覺得中國電影很有意思。

(　　) 1. What does Little Wang like to do?
　　　　a. Watching TV and listening to music
　　　　b. Watching Chinese movies and dancing
　　　　c. Watching American movies and singing
　　　　d. Playing ball and reading

(　　) 2. What does Little Li like to do?
　　　　a. Watching TV and listening to music
　　　　b. Watching Chinese movies and dancing
　　　　c. Watching American movies and dancing
　　　　d. Playing ball and reading

(　　) 3. Which of the following statements is true?
　　　　a. Little Wang and Little Li both like to watch TV.
　　　　b. Little Wang is American and he likes American movies.
　　　　c. Little Li is Chinese and she likes American movies.
　　　　d. Little Wang and Little Li know each other.

(　　) 4. If Little Wang and Little Li want to do something they are both interested in, where can they go together?
　　　　a. A movie theater
　　　　b. A library
　　　　c. A dancing party
　　　　d. None of the above

IV. WRITING & GRAMMAR EXERCISES

Section One

A. Use a word or phrase from each of the four following groups to make four sentences based on the Chinese word order: Subject + Time + Verb + Object.

    G1.   美國飯，球，音樂，電影

    G2.   明天晚上，這個週末，星期四，今天

    G3.   去看，去聽，去打，去吃

    G4.   我們，我爸爸媽媽，小白和小高，王朋和李友

1. _____ 。

2. _____ 。

3. _____ 。

4. _____ 。

B. Please use " (沒)有意思 " to complete the following dialogues.

  1. *A:* 你覺得昨天的電影_____嗎？

    B: 不，我覺得_____ 。

  2. *A:* 你想去看中國電影嗎？

    B: 不想。我_____ 。

  3. *A:* 你為什麼不聽中國音樂？

    B: 因為_____ 。

  4. *A:* 今天晚上的電視都很_____，我們去唱歌，好不好？

    B: 我不想去，我_____ 。

C. Please use « 因為...所以 » to answer the following questions.

1. *A:* 小高為什麼請小白看電影？

   B: _____ 。

2. *A:* 小張為什麼不想去打球？

   B: _____ 。

3. *A:* 小張為什麼不想去看電影？

   B: _____ 。

D. Please complete the following exchanges.

1. *A:* 你週末常常做什麼？

   B: _____ 。

2. *A:* 你喜歡看美國電影還是外國電影？

   B: _____ 。

3. *A:* 星期一晚上的電影有意思還是星期六晚上的電影有意思？

   B: _____ 。

4. *A:* 你今天晚上幾點鐘睡覺？

   B: _____ 。

5. *A:* 你覺得看書有意思還是看電視有意思？

   B: _____ 。

E. Translate the following sentences into Chinese using the words and phrases given in the parentheses.

1. Do you like going dancing on weekends? (V+不+V)

2. I often invite my classmates to go to see foreign movies. (請...去+V)

3. I like singing and listening to music. Sometimes I also like reading.

4. Because it was your treat yesterday, I'll take you to dinner tomorrow.
(因為...所以)

5. Little Zhang, long time no see.

6. Do you feel like going to play ball this weekend? (V+不+V，去+V)

7. I don't like reading. I only like eating, watching TV and sleeping. (只)

8. I think this foreign movie is very interesting. (有意思)

9. Then forget it. I'll go to bed. (去)

10. I am busy today. I don't want to go to see the movie. (想)

11. I don't like foreign movies. I only like American movies. (只)

12. Is tomorrow your younger brother's birthday (or not)? (V + 不 + V)

Section Two

A. List your hobbies in Chinese.

B. Describe in detail what you did last weekend.

C. Write a story which will include all five activities in the picture below.

Lesson Five Visiting Friends

I. LISTENING COMPREHENSION

Section One (Listen to the tape for the textbook)

A. Dialogue (True/False)
(   ) 1. Wang Peng had met Little Gao's older sister before.
(   ) 2. Li You was very happy to meet Little Gao's younger sister.
(   ) 3. Li You thought that Little Gao's house was nice and big.
(   ) 4. Little Gao's older sister works in a restaurant.
(   ) 5. Li You did not drink beer.
(   ) 6. Little Gao's sister gave Li You a cola.
(   ) 7. Li You did not drink anything at Little Gao's house.

B. Narrative (True/False)
(   ) 1. Little Gao's older sister works in a library.
(   ) 2. Wang Peng had two glasses of beer at Little Gao's house.
(   ) 3. Li You did not drink beer at Little Gao's house.
(   ) 4. Wang Peng and Li You chatted and watched T.V. with Little Gao's sister last night.
(   ) 5. Wang Peng and Li You left Little Gao's house at noon time.

Section Two (Listen to the tape for the workbook)

A. Dialogue I (True/False)
(   ) 1. The man and the woman run into each other in a library.
(   ) 2. The man and the woman have never met each other before.
(   ) 3. The man is looking for his younger brother.

B. Narrative (True/False)
(   ) 1. The speaker thinks that Little Bai and Little Li are old friends.
(   ) 2. The three people are most likely in the speaker's place.
(   ) 3. Little Bai told Little Li that he works in the library.

C. Dialogue II (Multiple choice)
(   ) 1: The dialogue most likely occurs in _____.
       a. a car
       b. a house
       c. a library
       d. a concert hall

(   ) 2. Which of the following statements about the woman is true?
       a. She doesn't like TV in general but she likes what is on TV tonight.
       b. She doesn't like TV in general and she likes what is on TV tonight even less.
       c. She likes TV in general but she doesn't like what is on TV tonight.
       d. She likes TV in general and she particularly likes what is on TV tonight.

53

(   ) 3. What will they most likely do for the rest of the evening?
      a. Watch TV
      b. Listen to American music
      c. Read an American novel
      d. Listen to Chinese music

D. Dialogue III (Multiple choice)
(   ) 1. Which of the following is the correct order of the woman's preferences?
      a. Coffee, tea, beer
      b. Beer, coffee, tea
      c. Coffee, beer, tea
      d. Tea, coffee, beer

(   ) 2. Which beverage does the man not have?
      a. Tea
      b. Beer
      c. Cola
      d. Coffee

(   ) 3. Which beverage does the woman finally get?
      a. Tea
      b. Beer
      c. Cola
      d. Coffee

E. Dialogue IV (Multiple choice)
(   ) 1. Where did they spend last Saturday evening? They were _____.
      a. at Little Bai's place
      b. at Little Gao's place
      c. at Little Li's place
      d. at Little Bai's brother's place

(   ) 2. What did Little Bai's brother do at the party? He was _____.
      a. drinking
      b. watching TV
      c. chatting
      d. dancing

(   ) 3. Little Bai spent most of the evening _____.
      a. drinking and watching TV
      b. chatting and watching TV
      c. drinking and chatting
      d. drinking, chatting and watching TV

II. SPEAKING EXERCISES

Section One (Answer the questions in Chinese based on the dialogues)
A. Dialogue
1. Who went to Little Gao's house?
2. Did Wang Peng and Li You know Little Gao's older sister before?
3. What is Little Gao's older sister's name?
4. How is Little Gao's house?
5. Where does Little Gao's older sister work?
6. What did Wang Peng want to drink?
7. Why did Li You ask for a glass of water?

B. Narrative
1. Why did Wang Peng and Li You go to Little Gao's house?
2. Is Little Gao's older sister a teacher? Please explain.
3. What did Wang Peng drink? How much?
4. What did Wang Peng and Li You do at Little Gao's house?
5. When did Wang Peng and Li You go home?

Section Two

A. This picture depicts a scene from Dialogue I of this lesson. Please act it out with some of your classmates.

B. You are talking with a classmate's brother/sister for the first time. Find out if he/she is a student, where he/she works, and what his/her hobbies are.

C. You are visiting a friend's room. Compliment the room. Your friend offers you something to drink, but you just want a glass of water.

D. Explain in Chinese that you went to a friend's house last night. Your friend works at the school library. You chatted and watched T.V. together and did not return home until 11:30 p.m.

III. Reading Comprehension

Section One

A. Please read the following description carefully and match each of the names with the proper beverage.

小高、小張和王朋都是同學，小高今年十九歲，小張今年二十歲，王朋今年二十一歲。小高不喜歡喝茶，小張不喝可樂，王朋喜歡喝咖啡、啤酒，但是不喜歡喝茶。

小高　　　茶

小張　　　啤酒

王朋　　　可樂

B. Read the following note, and answer the questions in English.

小張：

　　明天晚上七點半學校有一個中國電影，我們一起去看，好嗎？請你晚上來找我。

　　　　　　　　　　　　　　　　　　小高

　　　　　　　　　　　　　　　　　　七月五日下午四點半

1. Who wrote the note?

2. What time is the movie shown?

3. Where is the movie shown?

4. What date is the movie shown?

5. When was the note written?

Section Two

A. Read the passage and answer the questions. (Multiple choice)

　　昨天是小李的生日，小李請了小高、小張和王朋三個同學去她家吃飯。小李的家很大，也很漂亮。小李的爸爸是老師，他很有意思。他們七點鐘吃晚飯。小李的媽媽是醫生，昨天很忙，九點才回家吃晚飯。小李的哥哥和姐姐都不在家吃飯。王朋和小李的爸爸媽媽一起喝茶、聊天。小高、小張和小李一起喝可樂、看電視。小高、小張和王朋十一點才回家。

(　) 1. Where did Little Gao go last night?
　　　　a. Little Li's home
　　　　b. Little Zhang's home
　　　　c. Wang Peng's home
　　　　d. His own home
(　) 2. Who was late for dinner last night?
　　　　a. Little Gao
　　　　b. Little Zhang
　　　　c. Little Li's father
　　　　d. Little Li's mother
(　) 3. Which of the following statements is true?
　　　　a. Little Li's mother is a teacher.
　　　　b. Little Li's father is an interesting person.
　　　　c. Little Li's brother and sister were home last night.
　　　　c. Wang Peng talked with Little Li all evening.

B. Read the passage and answer the questions. (True/False)

　　今天早上小高去找他的同學小張，小張介紹他妹妹認識了小高，小張的妹妹也是他們學校的學生。小張的妹妹很漂亮，喜歡唱歌和看書。這個週末小高想請小張的妹妹去喝咖啡、看電影。

(　) 1. Little Gao met Little Zhang's sister before.
(　) 2. Little Zhang and his sister are attending the same school.
(　) 3. Little Gao's sister likes dancing.
(　) 4. Little Gao would like to invite Little Zhang and his sister to see a movie this weekend.

IV. WRITING & GRAMMAR EXERCISES

Section One

A. Please answer the following questions.

   1. *A:* 你常常在家看書還是在圖書館看書？

   B: _____ 。

   2. *A:* 你爸爸媽媽在哪兒工作？

   B: _____ 。

   3. *A:* 你喜歡喝茶還是喜歡喝咖啡？

   B: _____ 。

   4. *A:* 你爸爸喜歡喝美國啤酒還是喜歡喝外國啤酒？

   B: _____ 。

B. Answer the following questions based on your own situation.

   1. 你喜歡去同學家玩嗎？爲什麼？

   2. 你喜歡喝茶、可樂、咖啡還是啤酒？爲什麼？

   3. 你喜歡在哪兒看書？

   4. 你和你的同學常常一起做什麼？

   5. 昨天晚上你去沒去朋友家玩兒？

C. Please use each group of the following words to make an interrogative sentence, a positive sentence, and a negative sentence.

Example: 小高家 / 大

==> a. 小高家大不大？

b. 小高家很大。

c. 小高家不大。

1. 這個醫生 / 好

a. _____ ？

b. _____ 。

c. _____ 。

2. 小白的妹妹 / 漂亮

a. _____ ？

b. _____ 。

c. _____ 。

3. 張律師 / 高興

a. _____ ？

b. _____ 。

c. _____ 。

✓ 4. 那個電影 / 有意思

a. _____ ？

b. _____ 。

c. _____ 。

D. Change the following sentences from the positive to the negative.

Example: *A:* 我昨天晚上看電視了。

        ⟹ *B:* 我昨天晚上沒(有)看電視。

1. *A:* 他今天上午打球了。

    *B:*_____。

2. *A:* 我下午去小高家了。

    *B:*_____。

3. *A:* 上星期五是小高的生日，王朋喝啤酒了。

    *B:*_____。

4. *A:* 星期六他去圖書館了。

    *B:*_____。

E. Answer the following questions in both the positive and the negative forms.

Example: *A:*   你昨天晚上跳舞了嗎？

         B1: 我昨天晚上跳舞了。

         B2: 我昨天晚上沒(有)跳舞。

1. *A:*   小李昨天晚上喝茶了嗎？

   B1: _____。

   B2: _____。

2. *A:*   你上午喝咖啡了嗎？

   B1: _____。

   B2: _____。

3. *A:*   小白上星期回家了嗎？

   B1: _____。

   B2: _____。

4. *A:*   星期天小高去朋友家玩了嗎？

   B1: _____。

   B2: _____。

F. Translate the following sentences into Chinese using the words and phrases in the parentheses when given.

1. Let me introduce you. This is my classmate.

2. Very pleased to meet you. （認識）

3. Little Gao's home is very big and also very beautiful.（Adj.）

4. *A:* Where do you work? (在，哪兒)

   B: I work at the school.

5. Would you like to have some coffee?（點兒）

6. Would you like to drink cola or beer?（還是）

7. We got acquainted with Little Gao's older sister at the library.（在）

8. Last night they got together to drink and talk. （聊天）

9. Last night Little Zhang drank six bottles of beer.（了，measure word）

10. Little Bai does not like beer. He only drank two glasses of cola.

11. *A:* Why did you get home as late as twelve? （才）

   B: Because I went to see a foreign movie.

12. Last night Wang Peng went to Li You's home for a visit. He met Li You's
    older sister.

13. Let's go home! （吧）

14. Let's eat dinner! （吧）

Section Two
A. List what you drink in Chinese.

B. Describe a recent visit to your friend's house. Make sure that you mention what you
    did and what you drank.

C. Translate the folllowing note into Chinese.
    "Yesterday evening I went to the library to read. In the library I met a girl. She is
    very pretty. We read together, and I didn't go home until eleven o'clock.

Lesson Six   Making Appointments

I. LISTENING COMPREHENSION

Section One (Listen to the tape for the textbook)

A. Dialogue I (Multiple choice)

(   ) 1. Why does Li You call Teacher Wang?
   a. Li You cannot come to school, because she is sick.
   b. Li You wants to ask questions.
   c. Li You wants to know where Teacher Wang's office is.
   d. Li You wants to know where the meeting is.

(   ) 2. What is Teacher Wang going to do this afternoon? He is going to_____.
   a. teach two classes
   b. go home early
   c. attend a meeting
   d. go to a doctor's office

(   ) 3. How many classes will Teacher Wang teach tomorrow morning?
   a. 1   b. 2   c. 3   d. 4

(   ) 4. What will Teacher Wang be doing at 3:30 tomorrow afternoon?
   a. Attending a meeting
   b. Giving an exam
   c. Working in his office
   d. Seeing a doctor

(   ) 5. Where is Li You going to meet Teacher Wang?
   a. In Teacher Wang's office
   b. In the classroom
   c. In the meeting room
   d. In the library

(   ) 6. When will Li You meet with Teacher Wang tomorrow?
   a. 9:00 a.m.
   b. 10:30 a.m.
   c. 3:00 p.m.
   d. 4:30 p.m.

B. Dialogue II (True/False)
(   ) 1. Li You is returning Wang Peng's phone call.
(   ) 2. Wang Peng has an examination next week.
(   ) 3. Li You is asking Wang Peng to practice Chinese with her.
(   ) 4. Wang Peng is inviting Li You to have a coffee.
(   ) 5. Wang Peng is going to have dinner with Li You this evening.
(   ) 6. Wang Peng does not know exactly when he is going to call Li You.

C. Listen to Dialogue II very carefuly to see if you can locate the phrase which the curved arrow on the upper left corner is trying to represent.

Section Two (Listen to the tape for the workbook)

A. Dialogue I (True/False)

(   ) 1. Tomorrow will be Friday.

(   ) 2. Li You cannot go for the dinner tomorrow because she will be busy.

(   ) 3. Li You will be practicing Chinese this evening.

(   ) 4. Wang Peng promises to help Li You with her Chinese tomorrow at 6 p.m.

B. Dialogue II (True/False)

(   ) 1. The woman in the dialogue is the man's sister.

(   ) 2. The telephone call was originally not meant for the woman.

(   ) 3. There is going to be a Chinese film tonight.

(   ) 4. The woman will most likely stay home tonight.

C. Dialogue III (Multiple choice)

(   ) 1. Which of the following statements is true?

    a. The woman invites the man to join a dinner party at her home.

    b. The woman invites the man to attend a dance at her home.

    c. The woman hopes to join the dinner party at the man's home.

    d. The woman hopes to attend a dance at the man's home.

(   ) 2. Why couldn't the man go?

    a. He is giving a party.

    b. He has a test.

    c. He has another dinner party to attend.

    d. He has another dance to attend.

D. Dialogue IV (True/False)

(   ) 1. Wang Peng cannot help Li You practice Chinese because he will have class tomorrow afternoon.

(   ) 2. Wang Peng asks Miss Bai to help Li You with her Chinese.

(   ) 3. Miss Bai and Li You will meet at 2 p.m. tomorrow in the library.

II. SPEAKING EXERCISES

Section One (Answer the following questions in Chinese based on the text)

A. Dialogue I
1. Why did Li You call Teacher Wang?
2. Will Teacher Wang be free this afternoon? Please explain.
3. Will Teacher Wang be free tomorrow morning? Please explain.
4. What will Teacher Wang do at 3 o'clock tomorrow afternoon?
5. When will Li You go to visit Teacher Wang?
6. Where will Teacher Wang and Li You meet?

B. Dialogue II
1. Why did Li You call Wang Peng? Please explain.
2. Why did Wang Peng ask Li You to buy him some coffee?
3. What will Wang Peng do tonight?
4. When will Wang Peng call Li You?
5. Will Li You go to see a movie tonight? Please explain.

Section Two

A. You are calling your teacher and would like to make an appointment with him/her. Your teacher happens to be busy at the time you suggest. Ask your teacher when he/she will be available. Decide the time and place to meet.

B. You are calling a friend to ask for a favor and you promise to treat him/her to something in return. You would like to meet him/her tonight, but he/she is going to see a movie and does not know when he/she will be back. He/she promises that he/she will give you a call when he/she comes back.

C. You are calling a friend to ask a favor. Your friend is willing to help you. Decide the time and place to meet, and promise that you will take your friend out for a foreign movie.

D. Make an oral presentation in class describing this picture in detail. Feel free to borrow any sentences in the textbook. However, you are not allowed to look at the textbook when you make your presentation.

III. READING COMPREHENSION

Section One

A. Match the replies on the left with the appropriate expressions on the right. Write
   down the letter in the parentheses.

(　　) 1. 認識你們我也很高興。　　A. 你是哪位？
(　　) 2. 不客氣。　　　　　　　　B. 我們今天晚上去跳舞，好嗎？
(　　) 3. 再見。　　　　　　　　　C. 喝點兒酒，怎麼樣？
(　　) 4. 對不起,我不喝酒。　　　D. 喂，請問小白在嗎？
(　　) 5. 對不起，小白不在。　　　E. 認識你很高興。
(　　) 6. 對不起，我今天下午要開會。　F. 謝謝。
(　　) 7. 對不起，我明天要考試。　G. 明天見。
(　　) 8. 我是王朋。　　　　　　　H. 今天下午我來找你，好嗎？

B. Read the passage and answer the questions. (True/False)

> 李友是張老師的學生。今天上午李友給張老師打電話，因為她下個星期考試，想問張老師幾個問題。可是張老師今天下午有課，沒有時間見李友。張老師明天上午要開會，下午有兩節課，三點半以後才有空。張老師說李友可以四點以後到辦公室去找他。

(　　) 1. 今天上午 張老師給李友打電話。
(　　) 2. 張老師下個星期要給學生考試。
(　　) 3. 張老師今天下午要開會。
(　　) 4. 張老師明天三點沒空。
(　　) 5. 張老師明天下午四點以後在辦公室。

C. Read the passage and answer the questions (True/False)

> 小張今天很忙，上午有四節課，中午跟同學一起吃飯，下午在圖書館看書，跟小李練習中文，晚上到小白的學校看電影，十一點才回家。因為明天他有兩個考試，所以今天晚上他沒有時間睡覺。

(　　) 1. 小張上午有空。
(　　) 2. 小張下午不在家。
(　　) 3. 小張晚上跟小李一起練習中文。
(　　) 4. 小張晚上到小白學校的圖書館看書。
(　　) 5. 小張今天晚上不睡覺，因為他明天要考試。

Section Two

A. Read the following note and answer the questions. (True/False)

這是小王今天要做的事：

  8:00 中文課

10:00 去白老師辦公室

14:30 看王醫生

16:00 開會

18:00 跟小李吃飯

20:30 請小李喝咖啡

23:15 跟小張去學校看電影

( )1.小王今天只有一節課。

( )2.小王要跟小李一起吃午飯。

( )3.小王上午要找白老師。

( )4.今天晚上小李要請小王喝咖啡。

( )5.今天晚上小王要晚上十二點以後才回家。

B. Read this note, and answer the following questions. (Multiple choice)

小高：

    小張下午打電話給你了。他想請你星期四下午幫他練習中文，不知道你有沒有空。回來以後給他打電話，他的電話是324-6597。

                    姐姐

          三月八號(星期二)下午三點

(   ) 1. Who wrote the note?
      a. 小高。
      b. 小張。
      c. 小高的姐姐。
      d. 小張的姐姐。

(   ) 2. Which of the following is true?
      a. 小張星期四下午給小高打了電話。
      b. 小高知道星期四下午要幫小張練習說中文。
      c. 小高的姐姐請小高回來以後給小張打電話。
      d. 小高的姐姐給小張打了電話。

(   ) 3. Which of the following is true?
      a. 明天是星期四。
      b. 明天是三月九號。
      c. 三月八號是星期四。
      d. 三月十號是星期二。

C. Authentic Materials:

Below is a page of Little Gao's appointment book. Take a look at the things that he plans to do this week and answer the following questions in English.

1. 他星期天在哪兒吃飯？

2. 他什麼時候考中文？

3. 他跟王朋在哪兒練習中文？

4. 他姐姐的生日是幾月幾號？

5. 他星期五下午有什麼事？

6. 他請誰喝咖啡？

7. 他們星期幾喝咖啡？

8. 他們什麼時候喝咖啡？

9. 他星期天要去哪兒？

D. Take another look at Little Gao's appoinment book. Do you know what he is supposed to do on Monday morning? There is only character which we haven't learned yet. Please circle that character. That character was used as the phonetic elementary in another character in L. 4. What does the character mean in that sentence? Can you guess it's pronunciation?

IV. WRITING & GRAMMAR EXERCISES

Section One

A. Please fill in the blanks with appropriate measure words.

兩（　）問題

您是哪（　）？

三（　）課

四（　）茶 (cup)

五（　）啤酒 (bottle)

B. Following the example, make sentences using the given words and 得.

Example:為什麼今天晚上你不去跳舞？（看書）

==>因為今天晚上我得看書。

1.為什麼你不睡覺？（等我妹妹的電話）

2.為什麼你不喝啤酒？（下午上課）

3.為什麼你今天下午沒有空兒？（開會）

C. Please answer the following questions.

1. 誰常常給你打電話？

2. 你是大學幾年級的學生？

3. 你星期四幾點鐘有中文課？

4. 你星期一有幾節課？

5. 你明天有沒有考試？

6. 你知道不知道你的中文老師叫什麼名字？

7. 你喜歡跟同學一起去跳舞嗎？

D. Please use 要是 to answer the following questions.

1. 要是你明天沒課，你想做什麼？

2. 要是今天你們的老師請你們吃飯，你想吃美國飯還是吃中國飯？

3. 要是你明天考試，你想在圖書館還是在家看書？

4. 要是別人說謝謝你，你說什麼？

5. 要是你有空，你想去看電影還是想去打球？

E. Please use 但是 to complete the following questions.

1. 我想今天下午去找王老師，＿＿＿＿＿＿＿＿＿＿＿＿＿＿＿。

2. 我想這個週末去看電影，＿＿＿＿＿＿＿＿＿＿＿＿＿＿＿。

3. 我想請我的同學幫忙，＿＿＿＿＿＿＿＿＿＿＿＿＿＿＿。

4. 我想給你打電話，＿＿＿＿＿＿＿＿＿＿＿＿＿＿＿。

F. Rearrange the following Chinese words into sentences, using the given English
   sentences as clues.
   1. 四點 / 我 / 辦公室 / 電話 / 在 / 明天 / 等 / 以後 / 下午 / 你的
      (I will be waiting for your phone call in the office after 4:00 p.m. tomorrow.)

   2. 有人 / 不知道 / 請我 / 晚上 / 回來 / 什麼 / 時候 / 今天 / 吃晚飯
      (Someone is taking me out for dinner this evening. I don't know when I will be
      back.)

   3. 您 / 回來 / 給我 / 方便 / 請 / 以後 / 打 / 要是 / 電話
      (If it is convenient for you, please give me a call after you come back.)

G. Translate the following sentences into Chinese using the given words and phrases in
   the parentheses.

   1. This morning my teacher called me. (給，了)

   2. Teacher, are you free this weekend? I'd like to invite you to a dinner.
      (有時間，請)

   3. Don't go to his office. (別)

   4. When will you be free this weekend? (有空兒)

   5. This afternoon I went to look for Teacher Zhang, but he wasn't in his office.
      (可是，在)

6. Tomorrow afternoon I have two classes. I won't be free until after three thirty.
（以後，才）

7. This afternoon I have to give an exam to the first-year class. （要）

8. If it's convenient for you, I will go to your office to wait for you at 4:00 p.m.
Is that all right? （要是，去）

9. Because I need to take a Chinese exam next Thursday, I'd like to ask Wang
Peng to help me practice speaking Chinese this weekend.
（因為...所以，請，幫）

10. I'll wait for you, but you have to treat me to the movie. （但是，得）

11. I'll go look for you after I get back. （以後）

12. I'll wait for your call after I get back home.（以後，等）

13. Buy you a dinner? No problem!

14. Sorry! I will not be free next week.

Section Two

A. List the things that you need to do today. Don't forget to give the time.

B. Write a note to your Chinese friend to see if he/she can practice Chinese with you tomorrow evening. Promise him/her that you will buy him/her coffee afterwards.

C. Write a description of Little Wang's life. Little Wang is often busy. He likes to see movies, but he has no time; he also likes to listen to music, but no time, either. Tomorrow he will be free. He will take Miss Bai out for dinner tomorrow evening. He doesn't know when she will be back home tomorrow afternoon, but he will wait for her call.

Lesson Seven   Studying Chinese

I. LISTENING COMPREHENSION

Section One (Listen to the tape for the textbook) (True/False)

A. Dialogue I
(   ) 1. Li You didn't do very well on her test last week.
(   ) 2. Wang Peng writes Chinese well, but very slowly.
(   ) 3. Wang Peng didn't want to teach Li You how to write Chinese characters.
(   ) 4. Li You has prepared for tomorrow's lesson.
(   ) 5. The Chinese characters of Lesson Seven are very easy.
(   ) 6. Li You has no problems with Lesson Seven's grammar.

B. Dialogue II
(   ) 1. Little Bai is always late.
(   ) 2. Little Bai didn't go to bed until after midnight last night.
(   ) 3. Li You went to bed very late, because she was studying Chinese.
(   ) 4. Little Bai has a very good Chinese friend.
(   ) 5. Li You recited the lesson well, because she listened to the recording the night before.
(   ) 6. Li You has a very handsome Chinese friend.

Section Two (Listen to the tape for the Workbook) (True/False)

A. Narrative
(   ) 1. Mr. Li is an American
(   ) 2. Mr. Li likes studying Chinese, but not English.
(   ) 3. Mr. Li feels that English grammar is not too difficult, but Chinese grammar is hard.
(   ) 4. Mr. Li is having a hard time learning Chinese characters.

B. Dialogue I   (Little Wang is talking to Little Bai.)
(   ) 1. Little Bai didn't do very well on the Chinese test last week.
(   ) 2. Little Wang is not willing to practice Chinese with Little Bai.
(   ) 3. Little Bai is very good at Chinese characters.
(   ) 4. Little Wang can help Little Bai with both speaking and writing.

C. Dialogue II (Little Li is talking to Little Zhang.)
(   ) 1. Little Zhang usually comes early.
(   ) 2. Little Zhang previewed Lesson Eight.
(   ) 3. Little Zhang went to bed early because he didn't have homework last night.
(   ) 4. Little Zhang usually goes to bed before midnight.

II. SPEAKING EXERCISES

Section One (Answer the questions in Chinese based on the dialogues)

A. Dialogue I
1. How did Li You do on last week's test, and why?
2. Why did Wang Peng offer to help Li You with her writing of Chinese characters?
3. Who can write Chinese characters fast?
4. Which lesson will Li You study tomorrow?
5. How did Li You feel about the grammar, vocabulary and characters when she prepared the lesson?
6. What did Wang Peng and Li You do tonight?

B. Dialogue II
1. Why did Little Bai come so late today?
2. Why was Li You able to go to bed early last night?
3. Why did Little Bai say that it is nice to have a Chinese friend?
4. Which lesson the class is studying today?
5. Who did not listen to the recording last night?
6. How did Little Bai describe Li You's friend?

Section Two

A. Discuss the results of the recent Chinese tests with your friend. Comment on how you did on grammar, vocabulary and Chinese characters.

B. Find out why your friend is late or early for the class, and how he/she prepares for the new lesson.

C. Make up a story based on the two pictures below. Try to use the new words and sentence structures that you have learned in this lesson.

III. READING COMPREHENSION

Section One

A. Read Li You's schedule for Monday and answer the questions. (True/False)

早上	八點半	預習生詞
	九點	聽錄音
	十點	上中文課
中午	十二點	吃午飯
下午	一點	睡午覺
	兩點	復習中文
晚上	六點	吃晚飯
	八點	做功課

( ) 1. 李友星期一沒有課。

( ) 2. 李友星期一上午預習生詞。

( ) 3. 李友星期一下午聽錄音。

( ) 4. 李友一點鐘吃午飯。

( ) 5. 李友吃晚飯以後做功課。

( ) 6. 李友復習中文以後睡午覺。

B. Read the passage and answer the questions. (True/False)

小王：

　　你好！我上個星期有個中文考試，我考得不太好，老師說我漢字寫得不錯，可是太慢。中文語法也有一點兒難，我不太懂。這個週末你有時間嗎？我想請你幫助我復習中文。我們一起練習說中文，好嗎？

　　　　　　　　　　　　　　小白

　　　　　　　　　　　　　十月二十七日

（　）1. 小白上個星期考試考得不錯。

（　）2. 老師說小白寫漢字寫得很好，也很快。

（　）3. 小白覺得中文語法很容易，她都懂。

（　）4. 小白要小王幫助她復習中文。

Section Two

A. Read the passage and answer the questions. (True/False)

> 　　昨天是小高的生日，李友和王朋都到小高家去了。他們一起喝啤酒，聽音樂，唱歌，晚上十二點才回家，一點鐘才睡覺。因為李友沒有復習中文，所以今天考試考得不好。

（　）1. 昨天晚上小高十二點才回家。

（　）2. 昨天晚上十點鐘王朋和李友都不在家。

（　）3. 今天李友有個中文考試。

（　）4. 王朋和李友昨天晚上睡覺睡得很早。

B. Read the passage and answer the questions. (True/False)

> 　　今天上午，小李預習了第六課。第六課的語法有點兒難，生詞也很多。下午她要去老師的辦公室問問題。她覺得學中文很有意思。說中國話不太難，可是漢字有一點兒難。

（　）1. 第六課的生詞很多，語法也不容易。

（　）2. 今天下午他要去見老師。

（　）3. 小李覺得中文不難，可是沒有意思。

（　）4. 小李覺得漢字不太容易。

IV. WRITING AND GRAMMAR EXERCISES

Section One

A. Answer the following questions.

   Example: *A:* 你昨天睡覺睡得晚嗎？

      B: 我睡得很晚。

1. *A:* 你寫字寫得快嗎？

 *B:*_____ 。

2. *A:* 你妹妹唱歌唱得好嗎？

 *B:*_____ 。

3. *A:* 你哥哥打球打得好嗎？

 *B:*_____ 。

4. *A:* 她跳舞跳得怎麼樣？

 *B:*_____ 。

5. *A:* 你說中文說得怎麼樣？

 *B:*_____ 。

6. *A:* 你的老師念課文念得怎麼樣？

 B: _____ 。

B. Fill in the blanks.

  我和我的姐姐_____ (both) 喜歡聽_____ (music)。我們_____ (often)

_____ (together) 聽。我們____ (also) 喜歡_____ (study) 中文。_____

(however)， 中國人說中文說得 _____ (too)快。我 _____ (feel) 語法也

_____(a bit)難。

C. Complete the sentences with 才 or 就:

Example: 我們三點開會，可是<u>李小姐四點才來</u>。（才）
             我們三點開會，可是<u>李小姐兩點就來了</u>。（就）

1. 我們八點鐘有中文課，可是_____。（才）

2. 小王今天下午沒有課，所以_____。（就）

3. 我昨天晚上去朋友家玩兒，_____。（才）

4. 她媽媽說明天來，可是_____。（就）

5. 因為我今天有考試，所以我昨天_____。（才）

6. 我哥哥說今天晚上給我打電話，可是_____

_____。（就）

D. Complete the sentences with 因為 or 所以.

1. 因為昨天晚上沒有功課，_____。

2. 因為你有中國朋友幫助你復習，_____。

3. *A:* 你怎麼沒去看電影？

   B: _____。

4. *A:* 你為什麼請他喝咖啡？

   B: _____。

5. _____，所以他很晚才睡覺。

E. Fill in the blanks with 真 or 太.

1. 你這張照片＿＿＿漂亮。

2. 那個學校＿＿＿大了。

3. 今天的功課＿＿＿多了。

4. 這個工作＿＿＿有意思。

5. 第六課的生詞＿＿＿多。

6. 李友的媽媽＿＿＿客氣了。

F. Make sentences using the given words and 得.

   Example: 說中文 / 好 ===>他說中文說得很好。

1. 寫字 / 好

2. 說英文 / 快

3. 打球 / 不好

4. 學漢字 / 不太快

5. 喝啤酒 / 多

G. Translate the following sentences into Chinese.

1. The teacher writes Chinese characters very well.

2. Last night I was not back home until 10 o'clock. (就/才)

3. How come your younger brother didn't go to the movie on Wednesday?

4. She feels that Chinese grammar is a little bit hard. (有一點兒)

5. Because I am very busy, I will not go to the library until tomorrow afternoon. (就/才)

6. I went to the school (as early as) at seven o'clock today.

7. His older sister sings really well. (真)

8. You write the characters too slowly. (太...了)

9. I feel that the text of Lesson Six is a little difficult.

10. *A:* How come you are so happy today? (怎麼)

　　B: Because I did very well on the test. (得)

Section Two

A. Write a paragraph (5-10 sentences) describing your experience of learning Chinese.

B. List your daily activities starting from the time you get up and ending with the time you go to bed.

C. Write a paragraph in Chinese explaining the following: My younger sister did not learn Chinese well. She didn't like listening to the recording, so her pronunciation was not good. She didn't like studying grammar or writing the characters. That was why she didn't do well on the examination. But after she met a Chinese friend, they often practice speaking Chinese in the library. Now, she likes listening to the tape and writing the characters.

Lesson Eight   School Life

I. LISTENING COMPREHENSION

Section One (Listen to the tape for the textbook)

A. The Diary (Multiple choice)

(   ) 1. Which day of the week is August 10th?
  a. Monday   b. Tuesday   c. Wednesday   d. Thursday

(   ) 2. What did Li You do this morning before breakfast?
  a. She took a bath.
  b. She listened to the recording.
  c. She read the newspaper.
  d. She talked to her friend on the phone.

(   ) 3. What time did Li You go to the class this morning?
  a. 7:30   b. 8:00   c. 8:30   d. 9:00

(   ) 4. What did Li You NOT do in her Chinese class?
  a. Take a vocabulary test.
  b. Practice pronunciation.
  c. Learn characters.
  d. Study grammar.

(   ) 5. What class did Li You think was difficult?
  a. Chinese   b. Computer science
  c. American history   d. Economics

(   ) 6. Where did Li You have lunch today?
  a. At a Chinese restaurant.
  b. In the school's dining hall.
  c. At home.
  d. At her friend's house.

(   ) 7. What was Li You doing around 4:30 p.m.?
  a. Practicing Chinese.
  b. Reading a newspaper.
  c. Playing ball.
  d. Drinking coffee.

(   ) 8. What time did Li You eat her dinner?
  a. 5:45   b. 6:00   c. 6:30   d. 7:30

(   ) 9. What time did Li You return home tonight?
  a. 7:30   b. 8:30   c. 9:30   d. 10:30

85

(   ) 10. What did Li You do before she went to bed?
      a. Visited Little Lin.
      b. Did her homework.
      c. Talked to Wang Peng on the phone.
      d. Prepared for her test.

B. The letter (True/False).
(   ) 1. This is a letter from Yiwen to Miss Zhang.
(   ) 2. Yiwen's major is Chinese.
(   ) 3. Yiwen does not like her Chinese class at all.
(   ) 4. Yiwen's Chinese friend speaks very clearly.
(   ) 5. Yiwen is learning Chinese fast, because she has a Chinese friend.
(   ) 6. Yiwen would like Miss Zhang to attend her school concert.

C. Use numbers 1-3 to put the pictures in the correct sequence based on the information
   given in Dialogue II.

     (   )   (   )   (   )

Section Two (Listen to the tape for the workbook) (True/False)

A. Dialogue

(   ) 1. Li You is going to Teacher Zhang's office at 4:00 p.m. today.
(   ) 2. Wang Peng will be attending a class at 2:30 p.m. today.
(   ) 3. Li You plans to read newspapers in the library this evening.
(   ) 4. Li You and Wang Peng will see each other in the library this evening.

B. Narrative

(   ) 1. Wang Peng went to the library to help Li You with her Chinese.
(   ) 2. Wang Peng did not go to play ball this afternoon until he had finished his
      homework.
(   ) 3. Li You went to a movie with Wang Peng this evening.
(   ) 4. Li You has a Chinese class tomorrow.

II. Speaking Exercises

Section One (Answer the questions in Chinese based on the texts)

A. *The Diary*
1. When was the diary written?
2. What time did Li You get up on that day?
3. What did Li You do before 9:00 a.m. on that day?
4. What did Li You do in her Chinese class on that day?
5. Did Li You like her computer class? Why?
6. What did Li You do during the lunch hour?
7. What did Li You do that afternoon?
8. Please describe what Li You did that evening.

B. *The Letter*
1. Why is Yiwen so busy this semester?
2. Please describe Yiwen's Chinese class.
3. Is Yiwen making progress in her Chinese class? Why?
4. Why did Yiwen ask Miss Zhang if she likes music?
5. Do you think Yiwen has confidence in her Chinese? Why?

Section Two

A. Call your Chinese friend, and describe to him/her what you did yesterday at school.

B. Describe your Chinese class to your friend in great detail. Make sure to comment on how you feel about pronunciation, grammar, vocabulary, and Chinese characters.

C. Tell a atory based on the pictures below. Don't forget to mention the times.

III. Reading Comprehension
Section One (Answer the questions about the texts in English.)

A. *The Diary*

1. 這是幾月幾號的日記？

2. 李友早上開始聽錄音以前做了什麼事？

3. 今天上午李友有幾節課？是什麼課？

4. 李友中午在哪兒吃飯？

5. 李友下午在圖書館做什麼？

6. 李友跟誰一起打球？

7. 李友爲什麼去找小林？

8. 李友告訴王朋什麼事？

B. *The Letter*

1. 寫信的人叫什麼名字？

2. 你覺得意文喜歡她的中文課嗎？為什麼？

3. 上中文課的時候意文能說英文嗎？

4. 意文常常跟誰一起練習說中文？

5. 意文為什麼給張小姐寫信？

Section Two

A. Read the following and answer the questions. (True/False)

小張今天要做的事：

8:00	復習第七課生詞、語法
9:00	上電腦課
10:00	去王老師辦公室練習發音
14:30	去圖書館看報
16:00	去打球
18:00	去宿舍餐廳吃飯
20:15	給小李打電話，請他一起練習中文
21:30	寫信給爸爸媽媽

（　）1. 小張今天只有一節課。

（　）2. 小張跟小林一起吃午飯。

（　）3. 小張上午去見王老師。

（　）4. 小張去小李家練習中文。

（　）5. 小張吃晚飯以前去看打球。

（　）6. 小張去圖書館以後去找王老師。

（　）7. 小張睡覺以前給爸爸媽媽寫信。

（　）8. 小張練習中文以後才吃飯。

B. Read the note and answer the questions. (True/False)

小王：

今天晚上七點半學校有一個很好的音樂會，我想請你跟我一起去。請你回來以後給我打電話。我的電話是：八五七 九五六三。

小謝

七月五日下午四點半

（　）1. 電影七點半開始。

（　）2. 今天晚上小謝要看一個中國電影。

（　）3. 小謝没有電話。

（　）4. 小王下午四點半來找小謝。

C. Read the passage and answer the questions. (True/False)

> 小張今天很忙，上午三節課以外，還有一個電腦考試。中午跟朋友一起吃飯，下午在圖書館看書，做功課，晚上在電腦室工作，十點鐘回家吃晚飯。晚飯以後，他一邊看電視，一邊預習明天的功課，十二點半睡覺。

( ) 1. 小張上午沒空。

( ) 2. 小張下午不在家，在圖書館看報。

( ) 3. 小張晚上很晚才吃飯。

( ) 4. 小張晚上在電腦室預習明天的功課。

( ) 5. 小張一邊聽音樂，一邊看書。

D. Read the passage and answer the questions. (True/False)

> 小林以前常常跟朋友一起打球，聊天，看電視，不做功課。可是因為他下星期要考試，所以這個星期他不打球，不看電視，也不找朋友聊天，一個人到圖書館去看書。他很早就起床，很晚才睡覺，所以他上課的時候常常想睡覺。

( ) 1. 小林以前常常不做功課。

( ) 2. 小林常常跟朋友到圖書館去看書。

( ) 3. 小林這個星期除了不打球不看電視以外，也不找朋友聊天兒。

( ) 4. 因為小林不喜歡上課，所以他上課的時候想睡覺。

( ) 5. 這個星期小林睡覺睡得很早。

IV. WRITING AND GRAMMAR EXERCISES

Section One

A. Complete the following dialogues, and each sentence should contain a structure of double objects.

　　　Example: *A:* 他教<u>誰</u>中文？

　　　　　　 B: 他教<u>他弟弟中文</u>。

1.　　　*A:* 王老師教學生_____？

　　　　B: 王老師教_____。

2.　　　*A:* 小高給____一本書？

　　　　B: 小高給_____。

3.　　　*A:* 李友問誰_____？

　　　　B: 李友問_____。

4.　　　*A:* 高小音給_____一杯茶？

　　　　B: 高小音給_____。

5.　　　*A:* 你告訴王朋___了？

　　　　B: 我告訴王朋_____。

B. Follow the model and rewrite the sentences.

　　　Example: 他吃飯的時候聽音樂。

　　　　　===>他一邊吃飯一邊聽音樂。

1. 他聽音樂的時候看報。

2. 我們吃飯的時候練習說中文。

3. 我的朋友喜歡寫字的時候聽音樂。

4. 張小姐吃飯的時候看電視。

C. Follow the model and combine the sentences in each group into one that contains the
   structure "除了...還."

   Example: 我學中文。我也學日文。

   ===>除了中文以外，我還學日文。

   1. 我喜歡聽音樂。我也喜歡跳舞。

   2. 他常常打球。他也常常看電影。

   3. 今天晚上我想寫信。今天晚上我也想給我媽媽打電話。

   4. 明天我有一節電腦課。明天我也有兩節英文課。

   5. 他預習了生詞。他也預習了課文。

   6. 我喜歡打球。我也喜歡找朋友聊天。

D. Answer the questions.

   1. 除了中文課以外，你還有什麼課？

   2. 你常常跟誰一起去看電影？

   3. 你睡覺以前做什麼？

   4. 你起床以後做什麼？

E. Translate the following sentences into Chinese.

   1. My older sister taught me to sing, and I taught her to dance. (double objects)

      V IVO

   2. The teacher gave us a <u>lot</u> of homework.

      3

   3. I hope that you can go to the concert with me.

      叫好音

   4. We practice speaking Chinese while playing ball. (一邊. . .一邊. . .)

   5. In addition to pronunciation, Mr. Wang also teaches us grammar.
      (除了. . .也. . .)

      (049) option

   6. Wang Peng read the text very well. (complement with 得)

      V O V 得

   7. She wrote her Chinese diary poorly. (complement with 得)

      得不好

   8. When I went to see her, she was calling her boyfriend.
      (. . .的時候，. . .正在. . .)

9. *A:* I'd like to go to the dining hall to have lunch. How about you?
(到...去＋V)

   B: I had lunch as early as eleven. (就) I want to go to the library to read the newspapers. (到...去＋V)

10. He listened to the recording while having breakfast. (一邊...一邊...)

11. I take a bath before I go to bed. (就)

我洗了澡就睡觉

12. Li You dances very well, but she does not dance much.
(complement with 得；不常)

13. I go to class after breakfast. (以後)

吃了饭以後我去上课

14. When I went to Little Lin's dorm yesterday morning, she was chatting with Little Bai. (...的時候，...正在...)

Section Two

A. Write your friend a letter in Chinese telling him/her about your experience of learning Chinese. "My Chinese class is hard, but I think it is pretty interesting. My Chinese friend often helps me, and that is the reason my Chinese has improved rapidly. In addition to practicing speaking Chinese, I also play ball and go to movies with my friend. Both my friend and I are happy."

B. Write a piece of diary in Chinese about your school life.

Lesson Nine   Shopping

I. LISTENING COMPREHENSION

Section One (Listen to the tape for the textbook) (Multiple choice)

A. Dialogue I

( ) 1. What color shirt does the customer want to buy?
   a. Black   b. White   c. Red   d. Yellow

( ) 2. What else does the customer want to buy besides the shirt?
   a. A hat   b. a pair of shoes
   c. a sweater   d. a pair of pants

( ) 3. What size does the customer wear?
   a. Small   b. Medium   c. Large   d. Extra large

( ) 4. How much does the customer need to pay altogether?
   a. Between $20 and $30.
   b. Between $30 and $40.
   c. Between $40 and $50.
   d. Between $50 and $60.

B. Dialogue II

( ) 1. Why did the lady want to exchange the shoes?
   a. The shoes do not fit well.
   b. The shoes are damaged.
   c. She does not like the price.
   d. She does not like the color.

( ) 2. What color does the lady prefer?
   a. Black   b. White   c. Brown   d. Red

( ) 3. In what way are the new pair of shoes like the old pair? They are of _____.
   a. the same size   b. the same color
   c. the same price   d. the same design

C. Listening to the two dialogue in this lesson and decide which dialogue the pictures on
    the next page are depicting. Sequencing the four pictures based on the dialogue by
    using numbers 1-4.

97

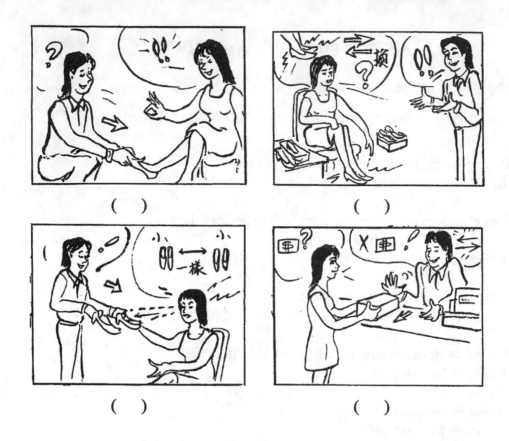

( )   ( )

( )   ( )

Section Two (Listen to the tape for the workbook)

A. Narrative (Multiple choice)
( ) 1. What color does Wang Peng Like?
    a. Blue   b. Brown   c. White   d. Red

( ) 2. Why does Wang Peng not like the shirt? Because of the _____.
    a. price   b. style   c. color   d. size

( ) 3. What colors are the shirts that the salesperson says they have?
    a. White, blue, and brown.
    b. White, red, and brown.
    c. Red, blue, and white.
    d. White, red, and yellow.

( ) 4. When did Wang Peng buy that shirt?
    a. 5 days ago   b. 7 days ago
    c. 10 days ago   d. 14 days ago

B. Dialogue (True/False)
( ) 1. The man returned his shirt for a different one, because he didn't like the color.
( ) 2. The man finally took a yellow shirt because he liked the color.
( ) 3. All the large-sized shirts in the store are yellow ones.
( ) 4. A large-sized shirt fits the man well.

II. SPEAKING EXERCISES

Section One (Answer the questions in Chinese based on the dialogues.)

A. Dialogue I
1. What does the lady want to buy?
2. Is the lady very rich? How do you know?
3. Please give the price for each item, and the cost in total.
4. If the lady gives the salesperson $100, how much change should she receive?

B. Dialogue II
1. Why did the lady want to return the shoes for a different pair?
2. Does the lady like black shoes? Please explain.
3. What color shoes did she finally accept? Why?
4. Did the lady pay any additional money for the new shoes? Please explain.

Section Two
A. Describe the clothes you are wearing today.

B. You are in a department store, trying to buy a shirt and a pair of pants. Tell the salesperson what color and size you want.

C. You bought a shirt that is too big. Try to exchange for a smaller one.

D. Describe the four pictures below without looking at the textbook.

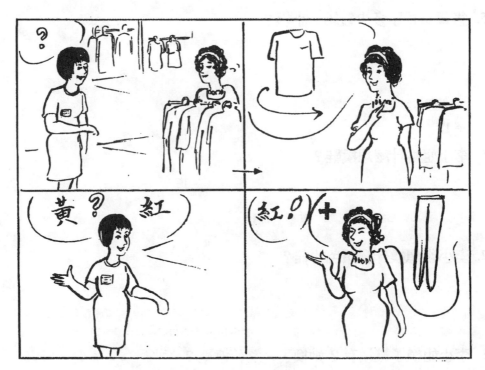

III. READING COMPREHENSION

Section One (Answer the questions about the dialogues.)

A. Dialogue I

1. 李小姐想買什麼東西？

2. 她買了什麼顏色的襯衫？

3. 她買了多大的褲子？

4. 襯衫一件多少錢？褲子一條多少錢？

5. 售貨員找了多少錢給李小姐？

B. Dialogue II

1. 李小姐為什麼想換鞋？

2. 李小姐想換什麼顏色的鞋？

3. 李小姐換了鞋沒有？她換了一雙什麼鞋？

Section Two

A. Read the passage and answer the questions.

上星期六，小張買了一條褲子，她想買黑色的，可是只有黃的和紅的。她買了一條紅的，回家以後，覺得不太喜歡那條褲子的顏色，她想明天下午去換一條別的褲子。

1. 上星期六小張買了什麼顏色的褲子？

2. 小張喜歡什麼顏色的褲子？

3. 小張為什麼不喜歡她的新褲子？

4. 明天下午小張要做什麼？

B. Read the passage and answer the questions (True/False).

李太太很喜歡買東西，她最喜歡買便宜的衣服。雖然她的衣服很多，可是都不太合適。李先生跟他太太不一樣，他不喜歡買東西，也不常買東西。李先生只買大小合適的衣服，所以，李先生的衣服雖然不多，可是都很合適。

( ) 1. 李太太不喜歡買貴的衣服。
( ) 2. 李太太有很多衣服。
( ) 3. 李太太的衣服都很合適。
( ) 4. 李先生有便宜的衣服，也有貴的衣服。
( ) 5. 李先生沒有很多衣服。
( ) 6. 李先生的衣服都太大了。

C. Find the corresponding clothing items to the expressions below. Put the alphabets in the parentheses next to them.

1. 鞋(　　) 2. 褲子(　　) 3. 外套(　　) 4. 帽子(　　) 5. 襪子(　　)

6. 裙子(　　) 7. T-恤衫(　　)

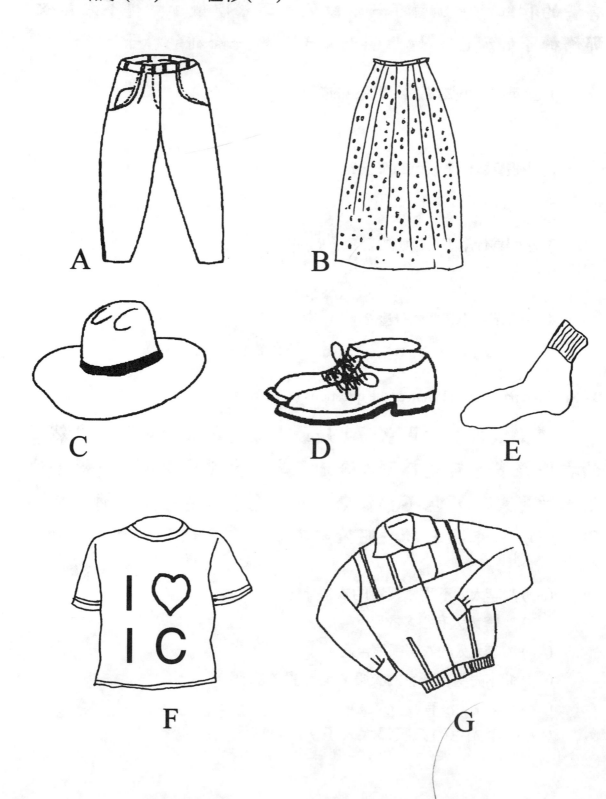

IV. WRITING AND GRAMMAR EXERCISES

Section One

A. Fill in each of the blanks with an appropriate measure word.

件，條，雙，本，瓶，位，節，封，篇，杯

1. 一（ ）鞋   2. 一（ ）襯衫

3. 兩（ ）褲子   4. 三（ ）課

5. 一（ ）先生   6. 一（ ）書

7. 一（ ）日記   8. 兩（ ）信

9. 一（ ）可樂   10. 一（ ）茶

B. Give Chinese characters for the following dollar amounts.

1. $5.12 _____

2. $18.50 _____

3. $70.05 _____

4. $99.99 _____

5. $100.60 _____

C. Complete the following sentences.

1. 這條褲子雖然顏色不太好，_____。(inexpensive)

2. 我雖然喜歡看電影，_____。(don't have time)

3. _____(very difficult)，可是我很喜歡學。

4. 雖然他上個月才開始學中文，_____。
   (speaks quite well)

5. _____ (I don't write well)，可是我很喜歡寫漢字。

D. Follow the model and complete the following sentences using the pattern "A跟B一樣
    +Adj."

Example：　我的襯衫<u>跟我哥哥的</u>襯衫一樣貴。（貴）

1. 這雙鞋_____。（大）

2. 學英文_____。（有意思）

3. 我的褲子的顏色_____。（漂亮）

4. 你說中文_____。（快）

5. 第七課的功課_____。（難）

6. 學校餐廳的飯_____。（好吃）

E. Complete the following dialogue.

售貨員：_____？
李小姐：我想買一條褲子。

售貨員：_____？
李小姐：大號的。

售貨員：這條太大了，你可以換_____。
李小姐：中號的很合適。

售貨員：_____？
李小姐：還要買一雙鞋。

售貨員：_____？
李小姐：黃的。

售貨員：一條褲子十九塊，一雙鞋十五塊，一共_____。

李小姐：_____。
售貨員：找您六十六塊。

F. Translate the following sentences into Chinese.

1. Would you like to watch TV or listen to music? (想；還是)

2. That large-size shirt is my older brother's, and this small-size one is mine. (noun/pronoun + 的)

3. The yellow shirts are expensive, and the white ones are cheap. (adj + 的; adj as predicate)

4. I want a shirt, not too large, and not too small, either.

5. The new words in Lesson Nine are not too many, and not too few, either.

6. Do you want to buy a pair of black shoes or a pair of yellow ones? (還是)

7. A bottle of beer is $3.00 and a glass of cola is 75 cents. $3.75 altogether.

8. This pair of pants are as just expensive as that pair.

9. The color of your shirt is the same as mine.

10. Although this pair of shoes fit me well, I don't like the color. (雖然)

Section Two

A. Write a shopping list in Chinese, including the names and prices of the items you want to purchase.

B. Describe what you are wearing in Chinese. Don't forget to mention color and size.

C. Translate the following passage into Chinese.
   "Yesterday I bought a yellow shirt and a pair of blue pants. The pants are very very expensive, but the color is very nice and the size is right. Although the shirt is very pretty and also very cheap, but it's too small. Tomorrow I'll exchange for a bigger shirt."

Lesson Ten   Talking about the Weather

I. LISTENING COMPREHENSION

Section One (Listen to the tape for the textbook) (True/False)

A. Dialogue I
(   ) 1. It rained yesterday.
(   ) 2. The weather today is better than yesterday.
(   ) 3. It will be warmer tomorrow than today.
(   ) 4. Miss Li will go to see the red leaves tomorrow.
(   ) 5. Mr. Wang went to Shanghai by himself.
(   ) 6. The lady suggests that the man stay home tomorrow.

B. Dialogue II
(   ) 1. It has been raining often recently.
(   ) 2. The weather will be better next week.
(   ) 3. This weekend is not a good time to go out, for it is going to be cold and wet.
(   ) 4. It will be hotter in two months.
(   ) 5. Little Ye is in Taiwan for a visit.
(   ) 6. The best time to visit Taiwan is in spring.

Section Two (Listen to the tape for the workbook)

A. Dialogue I (Multiple choice)
(   ) 1. What season is it now?
　　　　a. spring　　　b. summer　　　c. autumn　　　d. winter

(   ) 2. Where was the woman this afternoon?
　　　　a. In the classroom　　　　　　b. In the park
　　　　c. In the shopping mall　　　　d. In the office

(   ) 3. How will the weather be tomorrow? It will be _____.
　　　　a. cold and rainy　　　　　　　b. hot and humid
　　　　c. warm and sunny　　　　　　d. rainy and windy

(   ) 4. The man got the information on the weather from _____.
　　　　a. the T.V.　　　　　　　　　b. the newspaper
　　　　c. his friend　　　　　　　　d. the radio

B. Dialogue II (True/False)
(   ) 1. Wang Peng had an outing with Li You today.
(   ) 2. Wang Peng does not like the weather because it started to rain in the morning.
(   ) 3. The weather forecast says that the weather will be somewhat better tomorrow.
(   ) 4. Tomorrow Wang Peng will be preparing his lessons for Monday.
(   ) 5. Wang Peng believes that next Saturday it will be even cooler than tomorrow.
(   ) 6. The dialogue most likely occurred on a Sunday.

II. SPEAKING EXERCISES

Section One (Answer the questions in Chinese about the dialogues.)

A. Dialogue I
    1. What did the weather forecast say about the weather tomorrow?
    2. Was the man excited about tomorrow's weather forecast? Why?
    3. Where will Miss Li most likely be tomorrow?
    4. What did the woman suggest the man do tomorrow?

B. Dialogue II
    1. What did the newspaper say about the weather this week and next week?
    2. Why couldn't they go out to have fun this weekend?
    3. Please describe Taiwan's weather.
    4. Why is Little Xia not very familiar with the weather in Taiwan?

Section Two

A. Describe the climate of your hometown.

B. Compare the weather of your hometown with the weather of the place where you are now.

III. READING COMPREHENSION

Section One (Answer the questions about the dialogues.)

A. Dialogue I

1. 今天天氣怎麼樣？

2. 高先生明天想做什麼事？

3. 天氣預報說明天的天氣怎麼樣？

4. 高先生跟李小姐明天會去看紅葉嗎？爲什麼？

B. Dialogue II

1. 小夏怎麼知道這個星期的天氣都不好？

2. 台北夏天的天氣很舒服，對不對？

3. 小葉住在什麼地方？

4. 台灣什麼時候天氣最好？

Section Two(True/False)

A. Read the passage and answer the questions.

> 黃先生以前住在台中，台中的天氣很好，常常不冷不熱，很舒服。黃先生現在在台北工作。台北的冬天天氣很糟糕，不但很冷，而且常常下雨。他看報上的天氣預報說這個週末台北會下雨，可是台中的天氣很好，他想約夏小姐星期天到台中公園走走。

(   )1. 黃先生在台中住過。

(   )2. 台中的天氣很不錯。

(   )3. 黃先生喜歡台北的冬天。

(   )4. 這個週末台北的天氣比台中好。

(   )5. 黃先生聽朋友說這個週末台北會下雨。

B. Read the passage and answer the questions.

> 葉小姐一個人在加拿大的溫哥華工作，他的爸爸媽媽住(zhù:to live)在香港。葉小姐常常去看她的爸爸媽媽，可是她很少夏天回香港，因為香港的夏天又悶又熱。葉小姐想請她爸爸媽媽到溫哥華來住。可是她的爸爸媽媽已經習慣了香港的天氣，而且他們在加拿大沒有朋友，所以他們覺得住在那兒沒有意思。

(   )1. 葉小姐的爸爸媽媽常常來加拿大。

(   )2. 葉小姐常常在夏天回香港。

(   )3. 葉小姐的爸爸媽媽不覺得香港的夏天太熱。

(   )4. 葉小姐的爸爸媽媽在香港沒有朋友。

(   )5. 葉小姐覺得溫哥華夏天的天氣比香港好。

(   )6. 葉小姐的爸爸媽媽覺得住在香港比住在溫哥華有意思。

IV. WRITING AND GRAMMAR EXERCISE

Section One

A. Following the model, make sentences using the structure "不但...而且...".

    Example：漂亮 / 便宜

        ==>這件襯衫不但漂亮，而且便宜。

    1. 喜歡聽音樂 / 喜歡看錄像：

    2. 常常下雨 / 冷：

    3. 貴 / 顏色不好：

    4. 不便宜 / 不合適：

    5. 想去買東西 / 想去看紅葉：

B. Choose the appropriate adverbs to fill in the blanks. (真，太，又，再，更，很)

    1. 今天的天氣 _____ 熱了。

    2. 這個錄像 _____ 好看，我要 _____ 看一次。

    3. 這件衣服 _____ 便宜 _____ 好看。

    4. 上個星期的天氣不好，這個星期的天氣 _____ 糟糕。

    5. 我覺得寫中國字 _____ 有意思。

    6. 他喜歡看電視，但是他 _____ 喜歡打球。

    7. 他昨天給他弟弟打了一個電話，今天 _____ 給他打了一個電話。

    8. 這個地方 _____ 有意思，我們下個月 _____ 來一次，好嗎？

    9. 昨天晚上他不在家，我想他 _____ 去看電影了。

    10. 第五課的生詞 _____ 多，可是第六課的生詞 _____ 多。

C. Rewrite the sentences in each group into a sentence that expresses a comparison with the word 比.

    Example：昨天的天氣熱。 今天的天氣不太熱。

        ==> 今天的天氣比昨天涼快。

      or： 昨天的天氣比今天熱。

    1. 他這個星期很忙。 他上個星期不太忙。

    2. 中文很難，日文更難。

    3. 這本書沒有意思。那本書更沒有意思。

    4. 台灣的春天不舒服，秋天舒服。

    5. 這個地方的天氣很糟糕。那個地方的天氣更糟糕。

D.   Write a sentence based on the situation given.

    Example: Today's temperatures: Shanghai 95 degrees; Beijing 75 degrees
        ==> 今天上海比北京熱。
        or： 今天北京比上海涼快。

    1. Today's temperatures: Hong Kong 90 degrees; Shanghai 85 degrees.

    2. Prices for the shirts: yellow ones $16 each; white ones $18 each.

    3. Mr. Wang is 5'8"; Mr. Wang's son is 6'2".

✓ 4. Little Bai has 5 books; Little Li has 8 books.

5. Chinese is hard; Japanese is harder.

6. Lawyer Zhang is very polite; Lawyer Gao is not too polite.

7. The yellow shirt is not that pretty; the red shirt is very pretty.

8. Beers are expensice; colas are not that expensive.

9. Watching T.V. is not very interesting; going to the movies are really fun.

10. My father's office is big; my mother's office is not that big.

E. Complete the sentences and expand the dialogue.

A: 小謝，明天是星期六，我們去公園看紅葉，_____?

B: 好啊，可是我聽天氣預報說 _____。

A: 那我們星期天再出去吧。

B: 可是下個星期天的天氣_____。

A: 那怎麼辦呢？

B: _____。

F. Translate the following sentences into Chinese.

　　1. This shirt is both nice and cheap. (又...又...)

　　2. Summer in Taiwan is indeed awful! It is both hot and humid. (又...又...)

　　3. This shirt is not only very expensive, but also very ugly.
　　　(不但...而且...)

　　4. We can not only speak Chinese but also write letters in Chinese.
　　　(不但...而且..;會)

　　5. Li You wrote a letter to her mother last week. She wrote her another letter this
　　　week. (select: 又/再)

　　6. I called her yesterday, but she wasn't home. I will call her again today.
　　　(select: 又/再)

　　7. He went to a movie again last night. (select: 又/再)

　　8. It was very hot yesterday, but it is even hotter today. (更)

　　9. English is difficult, but Japanese is more difficult. (更)

10. The weather forecast on the newspaper says that the weather will be better next week. (會)

11. I didn't know how to speak Chinese before, but now I do. (了)

12. The weather is not good today. I'm not going to the park to see the red leaves. (不...了)

13. She was very busy yesterday, but she is no longer busy today. (不...了)

14. Eating Chinese food is more convenient than eating American food. (比)

15. The black shoes are more expensive than the red ones. (比)

Section Two

A. Describe today's weather.

B. Write 10-15 sentences comparing the weather of two of your favorite places. Be sure to use these expressions: 不但 . . . 而且 . . . , 又 . . . 又 . . . , and 比.

C. Give the Chinese version of the passage below:

I work in Taipei, but both my older brother and older sister are in Shanghai. The weather in Shanghai is different from that in Taipei. The summer in Taipei is somewhat cooler than Shanghai. Although the winter in Shanghai is colder than Taipei, it is a bit more comfortable there. I'd like to go to Shanghai to see my brother and sister this fall.

Lesson Eleven   Transportation

I. LISTENING COMPREHENSION

Section One (Listen to the tape for the textbook) (True/False)

A. The Dialogue
(   ) 1. Li You is leaving home for school on 21st..
(   ) 2. Li You should reach the airport no later than 8 p.m..
(   ) 3. Li You decided not to take a taxi because she thought it was too expensive.
(   ) 4. Li You didn't know how to get to the airport by subway.
(   ) 5. In order to get to the airport, Li You can take the subway first, then the bus.
(   ) 6. Li You finally agreed to go to the airport in Wang Peng's car.

B. The Letter
(   ) 1. Wang Peng gave Li You a ride to the airport.
(   ) 2. Li You cannot drive.
(   ) 3. There is bus service but no subway in Li You's hometown.
(   ) 4. Li You was busy visiting old friends.
(   ) 5. Li You felt that everybody drove too slowly.
(   ) 6. Li You enjoyed very much driving on the highway.

Section Two (Listen to the tape for the workbook) (True/False)

A. Dialogue I
(   ) 1. The woman has decided to go home for the summer.
(   ) 2. The man invites the woman to visit his home.
(   ) 3. The man and the woman will drive to the man's home together.
(   ) 4. Airline tickets are on sale now.

B. Dialogue II
(   ) 1. There is no direct bus service between the school and Little Gao's home.
(   ) 2. To get to Little Gao's home by subway, one must first take Red Line, then change to Blue Line.
(   ) 3. The woman decides to go to Little Gao's home by bus.
(   ) 4. There is a bus stop in front of Little Gao's house.

C. Dialogue III
(   ) 1. Old Zhang doesn't know how to drive.
(   ) 2. There is a highway going to the airport.
(   ) 3. Old Zhang will go to the airport with the woman.
(   ) 4. The woman will go to the airport by taxi.

II. SPEAKING EXERCISES

Section One (Answer the questions in Chinese based on the texts)

A. The Dialogue
    1. What will Li You do for the winter vacation?
    2. Has Li You made any travel plans for her winter vacation? Please explain.
    3. Please explain how to get to the airport from the school by bus and by subway.
    4. Will Li You go to the airport by taxi? Why?

B. The Letter
    1. How do you express New Year greetings in Chinese?
    2. Why did Li You thank Wang Peng?
    3. What has Li You been doing for the past few days?
    4. Is Li You a good driver? Please explain.

Section Two

A. You need to buy airplane tickets for your winter vacation. Call your travel agent, and reserve a ticket for December 22nd. Tell your travel agent that you prefer a morning flight.

B. What is the best way to get to the airport from your home? Are there any other alternatives?

C. Call your friend and thank him/her for the ride to the airport. Tell him/her what you have been doing since you returned home, and wish your friend a happy New Year.

D. Explain how to get to the airport from your friend's house by referring to the picture below.

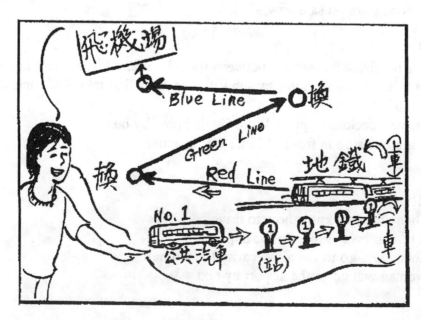

III. READING COMPREHENSION

Section One (Read the text and answer the questions in English.)

A. The Dialogue

1. 李友的飛機票是哪天的？

2. 李友坐幾點的飛機？

3. 要是李友坐地鐵或者公共汽車，怎麼走？

4. 為什麼李友說 "太麻煩了"？

5. 為什麼王朋不要李友坐出租汽車？

6. 你想李友最後怎麼去機場？為什麼？

B. The Letter

1. 為什麼李友覺得不好意思？

2. 李友回家以後，每天都做什麼？

3. 為什麼李友開車很緊張？

4. 為什麼李友開車很緊張，可是還是得自己開車？

Section Two

A. Read the following note and answer the questions. (True/False)

小李：

　　請你明天到我家來吃晚飯，因為明天是我的生日。
到我家來你可以坐四號公共汽車，也可以坐地鐵，都很方
便。坐公共汽車慢，可是不用換車。坐地鐵快，但是得換
車，先坐紅線，坐三站，然後換藍線，坐兩站下車就到
了。明天見。

　　　　　　　　　　　　　　　　　　　　小白
　　　　　　　　　　　　　　　　　二月十七日下午三點

（　）1. 小李要請小白吃晚飯。

（　）2. 坐地鐵去小白家比坐公共汽車快。

（　）3. 坐地鐵或者坐公共汽車都得換車。

（　）4. 小白的生日是二月八號。

（　）5. 坐地鐵去小白家一共要坐五站，還得換車。

B. Read the following diary entry and answer the questions. (True/False)

李友的一篇日記

　　今天是我第一次在高速公路上開車。我開車去小王
家找他去打球。高速公路上的汽車不但多，而且都開得
很快。因為我很緊張，所以迷路(mílù: to lose one's way)了。
我的車上有電話。我打電話給小王，小王告訴我怎麼走。
因為我迷路了，所以我很晚才到小王家。

（　）1. 李友常常在高速公路上開車。

（　）2. 高速公路上的汽車都開得很快。

（　）3. 李友開車的時候一點兒都不緊張。

（　）4. 李友可以在她的車上打電話。

（　）5. 今天的天氣很不好，所以李友迷路了。

（　）6. 因為李友迷路了，所以小王開車來幫忙。

（　）7. 李友去小王家，因為小王請她吃晚飯。

C. Find the corresponding picture for each of the expression below. Put the letter in the parentheses.

1. 出租汽車（　）　2. 高速公路（　）　3. 公共汽車（　）　4. 飛機場（　）

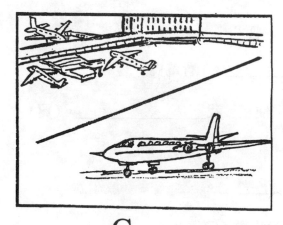
A

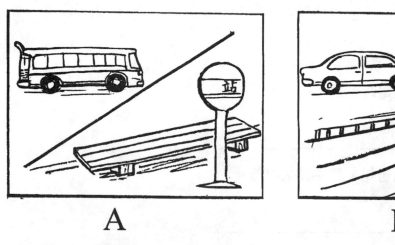
B

C

D

IV. WRITING AND GRAMMAR EXERCISES

Section One

A. Write sentences using "先...再...," based on the information given.

　　Example: 下課以後，他要去圖書館。

　　　==> 他先上課，再去圖書館。

　　1. 王朋八點吃早飯，九點上電腦課。

　　　_____。

　　2. 坐公共汽車以前，你得坐地鐵。

　　　_____。

　　3. 我十月五日去日本，十一月六日去英國。

　　　_____。

　　4. 他吃晚飯以後去看電影。

　　　_____。

　　5. 李友下午兩點去圖書館，四點鐘去打球。

　　　_____。

B. Complete the following sentences with "還是...吧."

1. 今天的天氣真不好，_____。（看電視）

2. 這件衣服太貴，那件雖然顏色不好，可是很便宜。我_____。（買）

3. *A*：我們今天晚上吃中國飯還是吃美國飯？

　B：_____。

4. *A*：明天又有中國電影，又有音樂會，你說我們去哪兒？

　B：_____。

C. Fill in the blanks with 或者 or 還是.

1. 他是中國人 _____ 美國人？

2. 到你家去，坐地鐵方便 _____ 坐公共汽車方便？

3. 你想買紅色的，黃色的，_____ 綠色的？

4. 今天晚上我想在家看書 _____ 看電視。

5. 我想要一杯咖啡 _____ 一瓶可樂。

D. Change the following sentences into the "topic-comment" structure.

Example： 她很喜歡那件襯衫。
==> 那件襯衫她很喜歡。

1. 我復習了昨天的語法。

_____ 。

2. 你買飛機票了嗎？

_____ 。

3. 我們都很喜歡喝中國茶。

_____ 。

4. 我很不習慣這兒的天氣。

_____ 。

5. 真不好意思讓你花錢。

_____ 。

E. Translate the following sentences into Chinese.

    1. It is raining. You had better stay home and watch video tapes. (還是...吧)

    2. *A:* Should I take the bus or the subway to go to the airport?

        B: You can go to the airport either by bus or by subway.

    3. You drive me to the airport tomorrow, can you?.

    4. I listen to the tapes every morning. (每...都)

    5. I have seen <u>that Chinese movie</u>.(topic-comment)

    6. Let's learn the pronunciation before we learn the characters. (先...再...)

    7. First, you take the bus, then change to subway. Finally you have to take a taxi. (先...再... , 最後...)

    8. It's too much trouble to write him a letter. Let's call him instead. (還是)

    9. You can go to the airport by subway. First, you take the green line, and then you change to the blue line.

Section Two

A. Describe your experiences driving or traveling on the highway.

B. Describe in detail how to get to the airport from your school.

C. Translate the following passage into Chinese.
   The winter vacation starts next week. In the winter vacation I will go home to see my parents. My dad bought me a plane ticket. (會) My mom called me yesterday. She told me that she had bought me three new shirts, a blue one, a red one, and a green one. I don't know whether I will like those colors or not.(V + 不 +V) Dad will drive to the airport, and my younger brother will go with him. I will see them at the airport. I talked to Mom on the phone in Chinese. (用 . . . V. . .) She said that my Chinese had improved. I was very happy.